DISCOVER
PATCHWORK

DISCOVER
PATCHWORK

40 ORIGINAL PROJECTS TO
BUILD YOUR NEEDLECRAFT SKILLS

TINA EALOVEGA

HAMLYN

First published in Great Britain in 1995 by Hamlyn
an imprint of Reed Consumer Books Limited,
Michelin House, 81 Fulham Road, London SW3 6RB
and Auckland, Melbourne, Singapore and Toronto

TEXT AND PHOTOGRAPHS © 1995
REED INTERNATIONAL BOOKS LIMITED

SERIES PROJECT MANAGER: **MARY LAMBERT**
SERIES PROJECT ART MANAGER: **PRUE BUCKNALL**
ART EDITOR: **ALISON SHACKLETON**
EXECUTIVE EDITOR: **JUDITH MORE**
ART DIRECTOR: **JACQUI SMALL**

PHOTOGRAPHS BY: **LUCY MASON**
ILLUSTRATIONS BY: **MICHAEL HILL**

The publishers have made every effort to ensure that all instructions
given in this book are accurate and safe, but they cannot accept liability
for any resulting injury, damage or loss to either person or property
whether direct or consequential and howsoever arising. The author and
publishers will be grateful for any information which will assist them in
keeping future editions up to date.

ISBN: 0 600 58591 3

PRODUCED BY MANDARIN OFFSET
PRINTED IN HONG KONG

CONTENTS

INTRODUCTION

Patchwork, like so many other needlecrafts, has enjoyed renewed popularity in recent years. In Britain alone, there are two national patchwork organizations, and currently four magazines dedicated to the craft. There are many patchwork shops that sell a wide choice of specially manufactured printed and plain cotton fabric, as well as special tools and gadgets. Modern patchworkers have now moved on from the old-fashioned methods of tracing around templates, cutting with scissors, and oversewing over papers. Instead they use rotary cutters which cut patchwork pieces quickly and accurately without templates.

Many people still think patchwork is only suitable for making bed covers, and that patchwork and quilting are synonymous, but the two can function as independent crafts. You can make unquilted patchwork, and you can quilt something that is not patchwork. And, as you will find in the following pages, you can make other interesting patchwork creations such as wallhangings, cushions, practical items for the home, clothes, and even Christmas decorations. There are projects in this book to suit every taste and every level of ability.

Patchwork is a sewing craft that involves cutting up pieces of fabric, arranging them in interesting patterns, and sewing them together again. Quilting is the stitching together of layers of fabric, usually with a filling of wadding for warmth. Often the quilting stitches form beautiful, intricate designs. This book concentrates on patchwork, but also covers quilting in some projects.

PATCHWORK ORIGINS

In Britain patchwork originated in the early eighteenth century when printed cotton fabric was expensive to buy and hard to find. Any scraps that were left over from dressmaking were saved to make bed quilts. The patchwork tops were quilted with sheep's wool to keep families warm in their cold, dark houses. It was a craft of necessity that was hand-sewn by candlelight.

In later years, with the onset of the Industrial Revolution, printed cotton was produced in Britain and became relatively cheap to buy, so patchwork changed from a subsistence craft to an art form. People also started to use sewing machines to make patch-

work. The craft continued to grow in popularity, in both Britain and in America. Today, most patchwork is machine sewn, because it is quicker and the stitches are stronger than hand patchwork. Because of this, all the book's projects are for machine sewing.

CHANGING FASHION

Over the years different patchwork styles came and went: eighteenth-century cut appliqué work, the crazy patchwork of Victorian times, beautifully stitched quilting patterns on whole cloth quilts from Wales and Durham and Northumberland, American-style piecing with its hundreds of named block patterns and Log Cabin patchwork all proved popular but went out of fashion. Then there was the hand-sewing method based on hexagons that was often taught in schools.

Many of these methods are now being revived and this book's projects show how to copy some of these older styles using easy machine-sewn methods and rotary cutting skills. Every item is clearly explained and illustrated with diagrams and the Materials and Techniques section explains the different patchwork methods in greater detail. You can learn how to make R.I.T. Squares: a special sew-before-you-cut method of doing machine patchwork. With R.I.T. Squares you can make items such as a cot quilt, cushions, a shopping bag and an oven glove and then go on to use the technique to make up your own designs.

If you buy a rotary cutting set and can sew accurately, you can try Seminole patchwork. The bright, colourful Seminole bands look more like weaving than patchwork. You can use them to make attractive gifts or household items such as cushions (*see pp. 58–59*) and curtains (*see pp. 94–95*).

You can also attempt Crazy Patchwork or Foundation Piecing and make some clothes or home accessories with these techniques. Both methods are excellent ways to use up your fabric scraps.

Machine patchwork is a fascinating craft that will give you hours of pleasure. You do not have to be an expert at machine sewing to make all the projects. Just start by making the easy ones and soon you'll be confidently producing useful items for your home and delightful gifts for friends and relations.

MATERIALS AND TECHNIQUES

In the eighteenth and nineteenth centuries in Britain and America, patchwork was a craft of economy and utility, especially among poor folk who lived in the country. Housewives carefully hoarded every tiny scrap of precious material left over from dressmaking, and when enough was saved the pieces were sewn by hand to make quilts and coverlets. Nothing was ever wasted. Even the quilt backs were pieced, and the wadding was often tufts of sheep's wool gleaned from hedgerows.

In those days, design in patchwork was dictated by the limitations of what little material was available. Keeping people warm in bed at night was its most important function. Nowadays, there is no reason not to recycle old clothes and scrap bag bits, but in addition to recycled material, fabric is available that is designed, dyed and printed especially for patchwork. Patchwork has been elevated from simple utility to an interesting craft. With an unlimited palette to choose from, the patchworker can let the design dictate the material, rather than the other way around.

BUYING PATCHWORK FABRIC

The best place to buy fabric for patchwork projects is in speciality patchwork shops. There you can find the best selection of prints and colours of the good-quality cotton dress-weight material that is ideal for the craft, as well as rotary cutting equipment, wadding, wider inexpensive fabric for quilt backs, marking pens and pencils, books and other items to help you in your work. Also, you will find that the shop owners are usually patchworkers themselves, who gladly pass on tips to customers.

CHOOSING PATCHWORK FABRIC
In *Discover Patchwork* details are given of how much fabric you need for each project. Unless otherwise stated, the measurements are given for 100% cotton fabric which is 45in (115cm) wide. For best results the fabric should have a good, tight and even weave.

Most of the projects need pieces that are less than ½yd (0.5m) in length. In ordinary fabric shops you can only buy material by the yard or metre. If you need ¼yd (0.25m) you have to

buy a long piece of material measuring 45in x 9in (115cm x 25cm). For patchwork, a much more convenient size is called a "fat quarter". A fat quarter is a ½yd (0.5m) of fabric cut in half the "fat" way to measure 18in x 22in (46cm x 56cm). Most patchwork shops have a big selection of pre-cut fat quarters to choose from, and will also cut fat quarters from the bolt for you if necessary.

Some of the projects in the book call for a "fat eighth" which is about half the size of a fat quarter, i.e. 11in x 18in (28cm x 46cm). These measurements are for your guidance only – normally the smallest size piece you can buy in a patchwork shop is a fat quarter.

If you want your quilt or patchwork item to be washable, it is very important to pre-wash and iron all cotton fabric before cutting piecing. This will guard against shrinkage and ensure colourfastness.

DIFFERENT FABRICS
Some projects are made from material not normally associated with patchwork, such as wool or silky fabric. If you are prepared to take extra care when dealing with bulky seams or shiny, slippery material, you can create a really individual item. There are no hard and fast rules about material you can use for patchwork, so let your imagination be your guide.

If you make a project that you want to quilt, you will need some kind of wadding. Wadding adds texture and warmth to a quilt, and a square of wadding under the patchwork top of a cushion cover makes it fit better on the pad.

Wadding comes in various weights and in different materials. For most projects the wadding used is made from soft polyester in the 2oz (50g) weight, referring to its weight per square metre. This lightweight wadding is normally bought by the yard or metre, 54in (140cm) wide, but is also available in patchwork shops in various large-sized pieces suitable for bed quilts.

For small items such as cushion covers that have been quilted by machine, squares of the mediumweight 4oz (100g) wadding are used. Although this heavier wadding is warmer and gives a nice high "loft" to your quilting project, it is difficult to quilt by hand.

USING YOUR SEWING MACHINE

Before this century, women sewed by hand, not from choice but because there was no alternative. With the invention of the sewing machine, seamstresses preferred to make garments and soft furnishings by machine, not only because it was quicker this way, but because the stronger seams created a much longer-lasting object.

In Britain, in particular, a patchwork tradition of sewing together hexagonal shapes had already been established before people acquired sewing machines. Hexagons, which need oversewing, are quite difficult to join by machine, so it was accepted that "hexagons" were synonymous with patchwork, and that machine patchwork was "wrong". A craftsperson might create a beautifully designed and technically well-sewn piece of patchwork, but be criticized because it was not hand-sewn or based on hexagons.

Nowadays, attitudes have changed and most people realize that good patchwork design is more important than how many stitches to the inch or centimetre you can hand-sew, and there is a real interest in finding new patchwork designs and methods. This is not criticizing sewing by hand. Always choose the sewing method and the design you prefer. For many patchworkers, a happy compromise for those who enjoy hand-sewing is to piece by machine and quilt by hand.

USING GOOD EQUIPMENT

Most of the projects in the book are pieced and quilted by machine, so adapt your particular sewing preference to the instructions given. There are, however, a few tips about making patchwork by machine that you should note. You do not need a modern, expensive sewing machine, but keep your machine regularly oiled and remove any fluff that accumulates in the bobbin case. You can do the most intricate piecing with an old-fashioned, straight-stitch machine as long as you can create an even, tight stitch that does not pucker and that looks as good on the back as on the front.

For patchwork made with ordinary dress-weight material, a sharp No.11 sewing machine needle is recommended. Unless the project instructions state otherwise, set your stitch length to 2.5mm or about 10 stitches to the inch.

PATCHWORK SEAMS

Unless otherwise noted for a particular project, all seams for the patchwork, whether sewn by hand or machine, are ¼in (6mm). The only real rule in patchwork is accuracy. If your seams are not all ¼in (6mm) the patches will not fit together, and, even after pressing, the blocks will not lie flat. So take care to sew an accurate ¼in (6mm) seam at all times.

The best way to gauge a ¼in (6mm) seam is by using a ¼in (6mm) foot, i.e. a presser foot whose sides are exactly ¼in (6mm) away from the needle. Many sewing machine manufacturers make a ¼in (6mm) foot especially for patchworkers.

Without this special attachment, there is another method of gauging the seam allowance with your presser foot. With many machines it just involves finding a point of light on the "toe" of the presser foot that is ¼in (6mm) away from the needle. Line up this point of light with the patch's raw edge, or with the diagonal line on a R.I.T. Square grid. If that doesn't seem to work, you can try "swinging" the needle a bit to the left or to the right.

Whichever method you use for these seams, please practise on a scrap of fabric until you can get it right. Remember that a tiny discrepancy on each patch makes a significant difference on a large project.

EVEN STITCHING

If you wish to quilt by machine, it is vital that the tension between the needle thread and the bobbin thread is correct. The stitches formed on the quilt back must be as good as those on the top, and a badly running machine may skip stitches or form loops. As quilting is a decorative technique as well as a method of holding quilt layers together, it is better to quilt by hand than to use a machine that can't form good stitches. Always test machine-quilting stitches on a sample "wadding sandwich" before quilting a patchwork project.

For straight-line machine quilting, better results are achieved with a "walking foot" or an "even-feed" foot. For free-hand, decorative machine quilting, you need a darning foot and the facility to lower the feed-dog of the machine (*see p. 17*).

(see p. 17)

TIPS

• Always adjust your sewing work table to the correct height for you, sit comfortably and work under a good light.

• Arrange your ironing table in reach of the sewing machine, or have a little pressing board and small travel iron right next to your machine, so that you can press your patchwork as you sew.

USING A ROTARY CUTTER

The introduction of rotary cutting equipment in the 1980s really revolutionized traditional patchwork methods. Before then, patchworkers had to trace around templates onto the fabric, carefully measuring seam allowances for each little piece and then individually cutting out the shapes with scissors. This method was not very accurate, it was very time-consuming, and it was wasteful of fabric.

Luckily for patchworkers, there are now rotary cutters, quilter's rulers and self-healing mats to make the chore of cutting out pieces for patchwork much easier, quicker and more accurate, without the use of templates. A rotary cutting set is expensive but is worth the investment if you get interested in patchwork.

A rotary cutter is a tool with a very sharp circular blade, a little like a pizza cutter, which can cut through several layers of fabric at the same time. Rotary cutters come in different sizes and grip styles, and blades are replaceable.

A rotary cutter must be used with a self-healing mat, which is made of a special kind of rubber that both protects the blade and provides a good surface for cutting. The mat is printed with grid lines to help you keep your pieces square. For your first mat, the most convenient size is 17in x 23in (43cm x 58.5cm); this is long enough to cut strips from a folded piece of 45in (115cm) wide fabric, yet small enough for the mat to be easily portable.

Please take care to store your self-healing mat flat and out of direct sunlight.

Transparent quilter's rulers come in all shapes and sizes, for slicing, chopping, trimming and measuring, but to start with choose a ruler at least 24in (61cm) long and 5in (13cm) or 6in (15cm) wide. You can use it as a straightedge and for measuring, and, together with the rotary cutter, it enables you to cut geometric pieces accurately without marking and without templates.

Most quilter's rulers are calibrated only in inches. Therefore it is strongly recommend that you use the imperial measurements given for projects in this book which use the quilter's ruler. (Left-handed patchworkers may find it useful to re-calibrate their quilter's rulers with a permanent marking pen, so that the measurements read from the left-hand side when they are cutting out.)

If you haven't used a rotary cutter before, it is a good idea to practise on a large scrap before cutting good fabric. Iron the scrap and lay it squarely on the mat. Place the ruler on top of the fabric so the right-hand edge of the ruler is just covering the left-hand edge of the fabric. The lines of the ruler should line up with the grid lines on the cutting mat.

First trim away the raw or selvage edge as follows. Pull away the guard protecting the blade of the rotary cutter. Hold the cutter at about a 45° angle and flat against the edge of the ruler as shown in Fig. 1. Press down hard on the ruler with your left hand to stop it slipping and push the rotary cutter forward, starting your cut before you reach the fabric and continuing past the fabric at the other end. (Left-handers should reverse this procedure: cut on the left-hand side of the ruler on the right-hand edge of the fabric.) After a few cuts you will feel how much pressure is necessary to cut cleanly in one go.

When you are making a long cut, you sometimes need to move your hand on the ruler to keep it steady along the cut. Leave the blade in the cut, reposition the ruler back onto the line if necessary, move your hand upwards on the ruler, and continue cutting.

USING A RULER AS A STRAIGHTEDGE
When you are cutting out R.I.T. Squares (*see p. 12*) or other fabric pieces with drawn lines, place the right edge of the ruler exactly on the

Use a rotary cutter on a protective self-healing mat to cut material easily and quickly. Transparent quilter's rulers can be bought in different shapes and sizes.

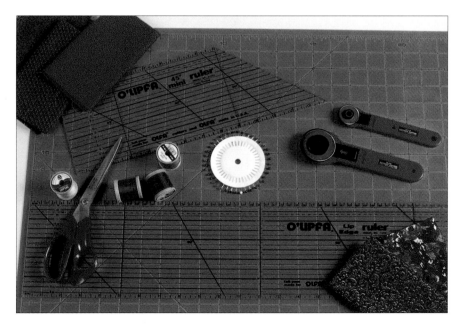

1

2

3

4

line you want to cut. First trim away the margins around the grid, and then cut out the patches. With R.I.T. Squares, make sure you cut on all the drawn lines (*see Fig. 1*).

MEASURING STRIPS AND SQUARES
If your piece of fabric is wider than your cutting mat, fold it in half so that the fold line is on the straight of the grain. Place the fold line on one of the horizontal grid lines of the mat with the edge you want to cut on the left. First trim off any raw edge as described above. Remove the ruler and pull the cut piece away without disturbing the larger piece.

To cut strips, move the ruler over the fabric with the trimmed edge aligned with the measurement on the ruler that you want to cut. For example, if you want to cut a strip 3½in (9cm) wide, place the 3½in (9cm) line of

the ruler on the left-hand edge of the fabric and cut. As before, be sure to avoid disturbing the large piece (*see Fig. 2*). Pick up the ruler and remove the cut strip before measuring and cutting the next strip.

To cut square shapes, stack up all your cut strips so they are even with a horizontal line on the mat and with the left-hand edges lined up. Trim off any raw edges on the left if necessary. Then move the ruler over the strips so that the measurement you want is lined up with the left-hand edge of the strips (*see Fig. 3*).

CUTTING ANGLED PIECES
To cut fabric pieces at an angle, lay the strip or strips across board and trim the left-hand edge as above. Place line of the desired angle, which is printed on the ruler, either on a vertical or horizontal line on the mat and cut (*see Fig. 4*).

No 1

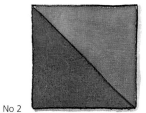

No 2

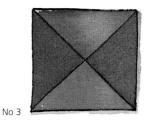

No 3

MACHINE PATCHWORK WITH R.I.T. SQUARES

R.I.T. (Right-angled Isosceles Triangle) Squares is a patchwork method designed especially for the sewing machine. It involves sewing triangular-shaped fabric pieces together before cutting them out, and is a very quick and accurate way to make the three types of patches shown on the left. You can then use these patches to create many different American block or border designs, or to build up patchwork designs of your own invention.

Many of the patchwork projects in this book use the R.I.T. Square method. It's much quicker and more accurate than old-fashioned patchwork methods where you have to trace and cut out all the pieces of material separately, and sew them by hand over little cards.

The R.I.T. Square method involves drawing a simple grid on your fabric. As in hand-sewn patchwork, you use templates to make R.I.T.

Squares, but the templates are really just measuring tools to help you draw the grids.

A 2-inch set and a 3-inch set of R.I.T. Square templates are reproduced for you to make 2in and 3in patches (about 5cm and 7.5cm) (*see pp. 108–109*). Even though the three templates that make up each set are different sizes, the patches all end up the same size, so that they are easy to sew together using a ¼in (6mm) seam allowance. You can produce the same block patterns with either size of template set; the 2-inch set is useful if you want a smaller scale of block or border.

To make the templates, photocopy the set you want to use or copy them onto tracing paper (*see pp. 108–109*), stick the diagrams onto stiff card, and then cut out the templates carefully with a craft knife. Alternatively, you can obtain the 3-inch set of R.I.T. Square templates in heavy-duty plastic, together with instructions and many pattern suggestions from Faberdashery (*see p. 112*).

HOW TO MAKE R.I.T. SQUARES

MATERIALS

No.1, 2 and 3 templates from 3-inch set of R.I.T. Squares

Five constrasting cotton fabric scraps: 1 4in (10cm) square piece for No.1 patch, 4 4¾in x 9in (12cm x 23cm) pieces for No.2 and No.3 patches

Ballpoint pen, scissors

Quilter's ruler, rotary cutter, cutting mat (optional)

Matching sewing cotton

Steam iron, pins

1 To practise the R.I.T. Square method, make this traditional "Ohio Star" block with one No.1, four No.2 and four No.3 patches. Make the No.1 patch by tracing around the No.1 template with the pen and cut out on the lines. Alternatively, use your rotary cutter to cut a 3½in (9cm) patch (*see p. 10*).

2 To make No.2 and No.3 patches, always remember to draw, sew and cut. Place two fabric pieces for No.2 patches right sides together. To make four No.2 patches, place two fabric pieces right sides together. Draw a line on the back of the lighter-coloured fabric about ¼in (6mm) from top (*see Fig. A*). This guide line keeps the grid square and is trimmed after sewing.

3 Place No.2 template up to the guide line and draw around it twice to make a grid of two squares (*see Fig. B*). Leave trimming margins at the fabric's edge. Draw diagonal lines from the corners of the two squares. Pin fabric pieces together in a couple of places and then sew a line ¼in (6mm) away from each side of diagonal line (*see p. 9 for gauging a ¼in [6mm] seam with a sewing machine*). At the end of the V-shaped line, don't cut the threads, but turn the work around 180° and then

continue sewing on the other side of the line (*see Fig. C*).

4 To finish the four No.2 patches, remove pins and cut on drawn lines with rotary cutter or scissors (*see Fig. D*). Discard trimming margins, and keep big scraps for other projects. Each square traced makes two patches because fabric is doubled. Open patches (*see Fig. E*) and press seams toward darker fabric.

5 To make four No.3 patches follow Steps 2 and 3 but use No.3 template, and draw two diagonal lines across each square (*see Fig. F*). Sew as Step 3, stitching on each side of one diagonal line in each square. Cut out eight small pieces on lines (*see Fig. G*).

6 Open up half pieces (*see Fig. H*) and press seams toward darker coloured fabric. Sort pieces into two mirror-image rows (*see Fig. I*). Taking a pair of pieces from

one row at a time, sew together, using a ¼in (6mm) seam so that darker triangles are opposite. Don't cut threads between patches, just sew up a long "kite tail" (*see Fig. J*). Cut four patches apart, pressing seams to one side.

7 Assemble Ohio Star block. Put nine patches down to form design (*see Fig. K*). With a ¼in (6mm) seam, sew patches together to make three rows. Press seams in opposite direction, then sew rows together, matching seams. To make other R.I.T. Square blocks, note the number of different patches in each block and multiply it by the blocks in the project. (With No.2 and No.3 patches you draw only half the patches needed.) Normally, the grid depends on the patch total and fabric shape. For example, you can make about 40 3in (7.5cm) R.I.T. Squares from two fat quarters (*see p. 8*). In each relevant project, there is a diagram showing the grids.

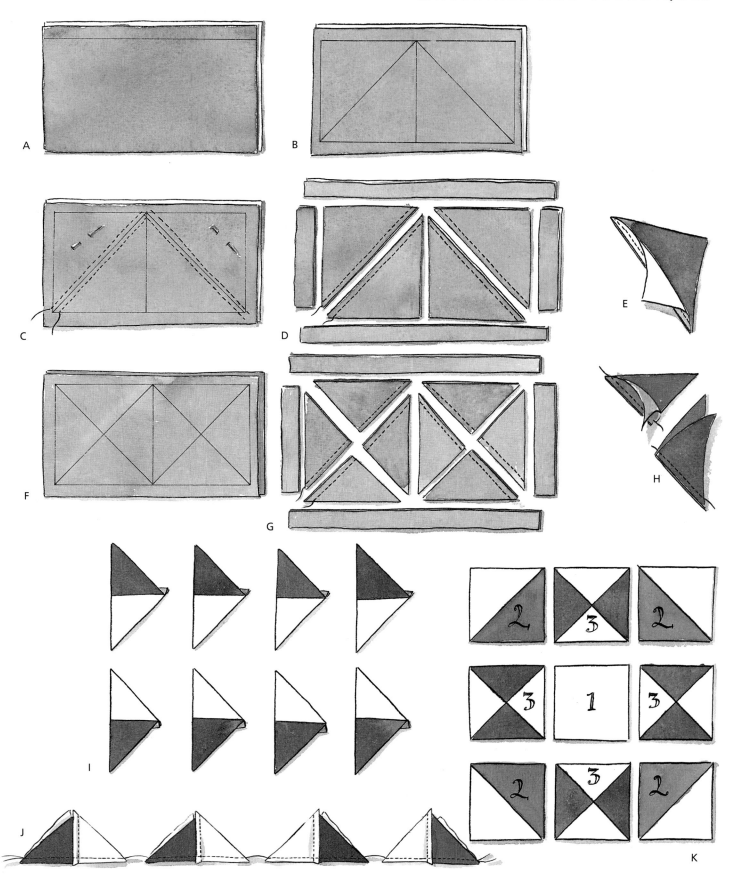

FOUNDATION PIECING

Foundation piecing is a method that takes you a step beyond R.I.T. Squares, because it allows you to join up odd-shaped pieces, and to piece very sharp points and very small blocks accurately. It also gives you a chance to use up all those spare little bits in your scrap bag and to cope with sewing difficult fabrics like silks and taffetas.

With foundation piecing you sew the patchwork pieces onto a background of paper or cloth which has the design drawn or printed on it. The foundation adds stability to the block, so you can piece lightweight or slippery fabrics with ease. You simply sew on the lines of the design and, with paper piecing, when the block is finished you just dampen and tear the paper away.

In this book we have included four Foundation projects for you to try: the Waterlily Cushions (*see pp. 60–61*), the Breakfast Set (*see pp. 92–93*), the Cottage Tea Cosy (*see pp. 98–99*) and the Pine Tree Christmas Ornament (*see p. 102*).

For paper piecing use lightweight translucent paper such as greaseproof paper. For cloth foundations, choose a lightweight but tightly woven fabric such as curtain lining. First photocopy or trace the foundation design onto a sheet of ordinary paper – this will reverse the image and your master design. Then cut the required number of foundation squares, making them about ½in (1.3cm) larger all around than the design. Tape the master design to the back of the cloth or paper foundation, place on a light box or up to a window, and with a ruler and fine-tipped pen, draw each copy. It is easier to draw on a cloth foundation if you first apply spray starch. Be sure to number the areas of the master, and of all the foundation squares.

Before you start sewing, place your iron near your work table, as well as a lamp without a shade and a bin for scraps.

CRAZY PATCHWORK

Crazy patchwork is easy with a machine and makes use of a mixture of silk, brocade, velvet, and other fabric scraps not normally suitable for patchwork.

1 Cut out a selection of crazy pieces in various geometric shapes that measure at least 2in to 3in (5cm to 8cm) wide. Then cut out a foundation base for the patchwork, which includes seam allowances, from a piece of mediumweight iron-on interfacing.

2 Pin a crazy piece in middle of the foundation's shiny side. Choose next contrasting coloured piece. Pin, right sides together, on top of first, so raw edges meet. Sew with ¼in (6mm) seam and finger-press outward. Each new piece must cover at least one raw edge of piece or pieces below it. Seam as above, or turn in raw edge of next piece on one or two sides and oversew. When fully covered, press (with cloth) to bond patches to interfacing. Decorate seams with hand or machine embroidery, if desired. Trim base edges.

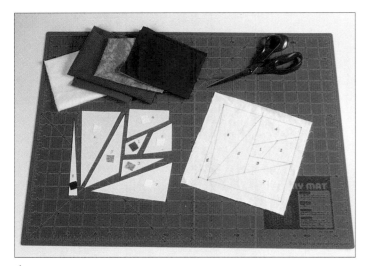

1

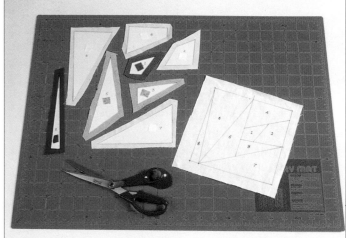

2

3

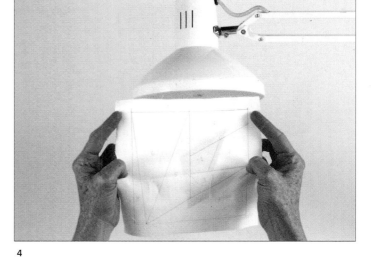

4

FOUNDATION PIECING METHOD

MATERIALS

Coloured fabric pieces

Paper foundations with design

Scissors, clear adhesive tape or spray adhesive, lamp, pins

Sewing machine

Matching sewing cotton

Steam or travel iron

1 Decide which fabric colours will cover each area of the design. As a reminder, tape a tiny swatch of each colour to numbered areas of your master design (see Fig. 1). Cut out pieces of the master design along lines in order to use each numbered piece as a template (see Fig. 2).

2 Stick each template face up with rolled-up clear adhesive tape on the back of correct fabric and roughly cut a piece at least ⅜in (8mm) larger all around than the template (see Fig. 3). If you are making more than one block, make sure you cut enough pieces for each one. (You can also temporarily stick the templates by spraying the back of the templates with some adhesive.)

3 Starting with Piece 1, remove the paper template, hold the foundation up to the light, and place the piece on the blank side of the foundation right side up so that it covers Area 1. Pin in place. Take Piece 2. Holding foundation up to the light, first hold Piece 2 so that it covers Area 2, right side up. Then turn it over Piece 1 so the edge of the paper template is on the line between Area 1 and Area 2 (see Fig. 4). Remove template and pin in place.

4 Turn the foundation over and sew on the line between 1 and 2. (Start and finish stitching just a little beyond the line.) From the right side of the foundation again, remove the pin and fold Piece 2 back along the seam line, checking with the light that you have completely covered Area 2. Then fold the piece back and trim the seam to about ¼in (6mm). Press Piece 2 right side out again.

5 Take the next piece and repeat Steps 3 and 4 until all the pieces have been sewn on. Sew all around the block about ⅛in (3mm) outside the marked line. Join blocks together, or attach borders, by sewing on the lines around the blocks. Stick pins through at the corners to make sure that the corners and lines align. If you are using a paper foundation, tear it away from the block. (This is easier if you dampen it first.)

QUILTING

Quilting is the technique of holding together layers of cloth, usually with a filling of wadding, either by working utilitarian straight-lines running stitches or by decorative stitching, by hand or by machine. Quilting your patchwork project is not necessary, but it adds an extra dimension to your work.

Another way of holding layers of patchwork together is by "tying" (*see Four-Patch Quilt pp. 24–25*). Patchwork and quilting are really two separate crafts that are often combined to make "patchwork quilts".

Many modern patchworkers make a happy compromise between machine sewing and hand work by piecing by machine and quilting by hand. Hand quilting is very relaxing, and it is satisfying to see your beautiful quilting patterns building up. Machine quilting, which is much quicker and enables you to quilt easily over bulky seams, requires some practice.

Before quilting you need to prepare the quilt or other project by tacking the top layer together with the wadding and the backing fabric (*see p. 19*). Decide which areas of your patchwork project you want to quilt. You may decide to quilt in straight lines around the patches of a patchwork block or border to add texture to the design. With hand quilting this is usually done by stitching about ¼in (6mm) away from the seam, so you avoid the bulk of sewing though the extra layers. With machine quilting, you can sew right in the seam line.

Alternatively, you might like to try a fancy quilting design. Choose one that fits the area you want to quilt and that enhances the patchwork. You can either buy a ready-cut quilting stencil from a patchwork shop, or you can make your own from a design you have drawn or copied from a patchwork book. Designs for hand quilting should be smooth and flowing and not too intricate.

Designs for machine quilting can be much more intricate, but should have continuous lines with as few starts and stops as possible (*see Flying Geese Throw pp. 30–31, and Jacob's Ladder Cot Quilt pp. 34–35*).

When hand quilting, it is easier to stitch fancy quilting designs on plain blocks or borders rather than over pieced areas of the design. Also, quilting shows up much better on plain fabric than on prints. For example, look at the Nine-patch Quilt on pages 28–29 and the Quilted Amish Picture on pages 82–83. The central diamond between the patchwork blocks is perfect for a hand-quilting design.

MAKING A QUILTING STENCIL

A purchased quilting stencil has channels cut out around the design, through which you mark the fabric. To make your own stencil, you need a sheet of tough, but thin, transparent plastic just larger than your chosen design. Enlarge or reduce your design, if necessary, by photocopying and tape to the back of the stencil plastic. With needle pricks about ⅛in (3mm) apart, make holes by hand or machine through the lines of the design. If using a machine, remove thread from needle and bobbin and prick through with a No.16 needle.

MAKING A "POUNCE" BAG

To make marks on the fabric through the pricked holes in your stencil, you will need a pounce bag. Cut a piece of loosely woven material about 4in (10cm) square. To mark on dark-coloured fabrics, place about a teaspoonful of cornflour in the middle of the square and tie up the square to make a bag. To mark light-coloured fabrics, use ground cinnamon.

For drawing quilting designs you need a marker that draws on fabric without dragging and has a clear line that is easy to remove after quilting. You can find all sorts of markers in speciality patchwork shops such as white, yellow, or silver pencils to mark on dark-coloured fabric, and water-erasable pens for lighter fabrics.

TRANSFERRING THE DESIGN

To transfer your design onto a quilt, you need your quilting stencil, a pounce bag (only if you are using your own, pricked stencil), and a marking pen or pencil.

Place the quilting stencil over the area to be quilted and hold in place with adhesive tape. If you are using a pricked stencil, pounce through the design by bouncing the pounce bag against the stencil so that the dust penetrates the holes or channels and forms tiny dots on the fabric's surface. Remove stencil, and draw over pounced design with your marker. With a bought stencil, just use the marker to draw the design. Straight lines can be marked with a marker or with ¼in (6mm) masking tape (available from patchwork shops).

HAND QUILTING

You need short, fine size 10 or 12 quilting needles, quilting thread (which is slightly heavier than ordinary sewing cotton), two thimbles (one for your sewing hand and one to stop the needle pricking your other hand), and a quilting hoop.

Place the area to be quilted in a quilting hoop to hold the fabric taut. Thread the needle with a short length of quilting thread and make a small knot. The thread is usually the same colour as the background, but you can choose a contrasting colour for extra impact. At the beginning of the quilting design, pull the thread through from the back and "pop" the knot through just the back layer of fabric. Taking short stitches through all the layers of fabric, load the needle with several stitches at a time before pulling the thread through. At the end of the design, tie off the thread and hide the end in the wadding.

MACHINE QUILTING

There are two ways of quilting by machine – either straight-line quilting, which is a more utilitarian technique, or fancy quilting which is done with free-motion stitching.

STRAIGHT-LINE MACHINE QUILTING

Most of the patchwork projects in this book are machine quilted with straight-line quilting. There is a sewing-machine attachment called a "walking foot" or an "even-feed" foot, available from your sewing machine dealer, which works by feeding the top layer of fabric under the foot at the same time as the bottom layer. You should use a walking foot for straight-line machine quilting if possible to avoid any puckering and pulling of the fabric.

After putting together your quilt (*see p. 19*), study the patchwork and decide where the design can be enhanced by a line of quilting. Thread the needle with a sewing cotton to blend with the patchwork's colours, and fill the bobbin with a colour to match the back. If you are quilting over many different colours, you can use transparent nylon quilting thread in the needle.

Set the stitch length to about 10 stitches to an inch or 2.5mm and check your stitches on a little sample "wadding sandwich" to make sure that the tension is correct. Begin by making several stitches in place in order to lock the stitches and then sew along your planned route, keeping close to the seam lines, but on the flatter side opposite to which the seams have been pressed. This technique is called "stitch-in-the-ditch". When you come to a corner, put the needle in the down position, turn and continue sewing. Try to plan a route with as few starts and stops as possible. When you get to the end, stitch in place as before and clip the thread ends close to the work.

When you are quilting the middle of a large item, such as a bed quilt, roll up the sides tightly and hold it in place with bicycle clips.

FANCY MACHINE QUILTING

Once you have got used to freehand quilting, you will find that you can easily quilt quite intricate designs and you can easily move the fabric in any direction.

Thread the machine as for straight-line quilting. Before you begin, read the instructions in your sewing machine manual about darning. It is not possible to do freehand machine quilting with an ordinary presser foot, so replace this with a darning foot that allows free movement of fabric beneath it. Also lower or cover the feed-dog.

Practise free-motion quilting on a sample "wadding sandwich" and do the following exercises until you feel confident about trying machine quilting on your patchwork. First, grip the sandwich firmly with both hands and sew some free-hand "squiggles" and loops by moving the sandwich round and round under the needle. You will soon discover how to form even stitches and smooth curves by varying the speed with which you move the fabric under the needle, and how fast you run the machine. Next draw a quilting pattern on the wadding sandwich. Practise as above, trying to keep the stitches on the pattern lines. However, it is more important to keep your quilting line smooth. Fix the stitches at the top and bottom of the designs by sewing a few stitches in place. Occasionally check the tension at the back.

Remember, you can move the fabric in any direction under the needle, so when you get to the end of a curve leave the needle down and turn the work for you to see your next line. If you wear lightweight rubber gloves for free-hand quilting, you can grip the quilt more easily.

A continuous line design for freehand machine quilting, seen opposite, is used in the Flying Geese Throw (see pp. 30–31). The line design above features in the Jacob's Ladder Cot Quilt (see pp. 34–35).

A typical hand-quilting design that decorates the Quilted Amish Picture (see pp. 82–83).

A hand-quilting design in Jacob's Ladder Cot Quilt (see pp. 34–35).

PRESSING AND "BLOCKING" PATCHWORK

Your iron is as important a tool as your sewing machine for neat and accurate patchwork. Always set up your ironing table near the sewing machine so that it will be easy for you to press your patchwork pieces as you sew.

Before you cut or mark fabric, it is important to press it. If your fabric is rather flimsy, a treatment with spray starch makes cutting and piecing easier.

PRESSING SEAMS

Generally speaking, in patchwork you do not have to press seams open, but toward the darker side of the seam. Also, when sewing rows of patches together, avoid bulky seams wherever possible by pressing the seams of alternate rows of patches in opposite directions (*see Fig. A*). In doing this, you will sometimes have to break the rule about always pressing

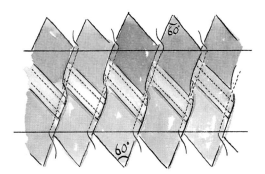

seams toward the darker side.

With some patchwork blocks, whichever way you press, it is impossible to avoid lots of seams converging in the same place. To reduce the bulk in this situation, you can sometimes clip the seams so that they change direction (*see Fig. B*).

BLOCKING

It is a good idea to draw a grid on your ironing table cover as an aid to pressing and blocking. It almost always happens, however carefully and accurately you sew, that long rows or borders of patches end up being rather crooked. It is important to block the patchwork row before you continue sewing.

Lay the row or border on the ironing table so that it is lined up with one of your grid lines (*see Fig. 1*). Pin the row in place along the top and bottom into the pad of the table surface. Press down firmly with a steam iron to straighten the row firmly against the grid line (*see Fig. 2*).

PUTTING TOGETHER THE LAYERS OF A QUILT

Before quilting or tying your quilt, and before putting on the binding, you must secure together the patchwork top, the wadding and the backing fabric by making a "quilt sandwich". The usual way to do this is by tacking. Press the top and back well to

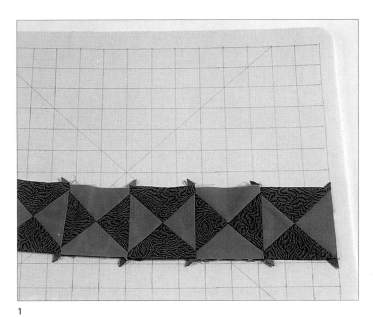

1

2

eliminate any wrinkles or creases. Cut the back
a little larger all around than the patchwork
and lay it face down on the floor. Cut a piece
of wadding the same size and lay it on top of
the back. Centre the top over the wadding,
smoothing out the layers to avoid any
unsightly wrinkling.

Tack the three layers together as follows.
Thread a long needle and stitch from the
middle of the quilt diagonally out to the
corners. Then make a grid of horizontal and
vertical lines. The tacking lines should be at
least 6in (15cm) apart.

Tack all around the edge too (*see Fig. A*). If
your machine has a zig-zag stitch, it is a good
idea to zig-zag all around the raw edges of the
top. You are now ready to start quilting, either
by hand or machine.

USING "STICKY WADDING"
Another way of securing quilt layers together is
called "sticky wadding", and is ideal for
machine quilting. With this method you can
actually glue the layers together with spray
adhesive (available from graphic art shops).

Prepare the patchwork, back and wadding
as above. First protect the floor with a large
plastic sheet, and open windows to provide
good ventilation. Lay the wadding on the
sheet. Lay a length of dark thread across the
middle of the wadding in both directions.
Hold the thread in place by winding around a
pin at each end.

Spray the wadding all over with the
adhesive. Place right sides together, fold the
patchwork top in half first one way and then
the other way. Lay the folded edges up to the
thread lines on one quarter of the wadding and
then drop the patchwork onto the sticky
surface (*see Fig. B*). You will need a friend to
help you if your quilt is very large. Unfold the
patchwork onto the rest of the wadding,
smoothing down any unattractive wrinkles
with your hand. (You can lift the patchwork
up and lay it down again if any puckers do
start to appear.)

Repeat this procedure with the backing
fabric. You may find it necessary to pin all
around the edges before zig-zagging around the
raw edges of the top.

Trim away any excess wadding and backing
fabric up to the zig-zag line. Quilt in your
pattern as desired (*see pp. 16–17*).

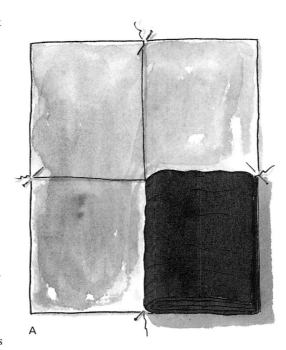

A

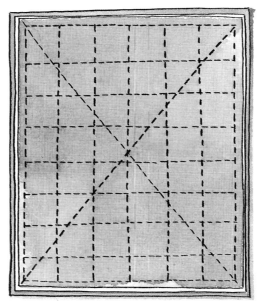

B

BINDING A QUILT

Here is a simple method of binding a quilt with one fabric strip. The corners are folded in using a method that produces a neat mitre. The binding is sewn first to the back of the quilt by machine. It is then folded over to the front, and this edge is either sewn down with tiny zig-zag machine stitches, or by hand using blind-stitching. You do not have to cut binding for a quilt on the bias unless the quilt edge itself is curved.

A

B

C

D

E

F

G

H

SEWING ON A BINDING

MATERIALS
Fabric strips for binding
Sewing machine
Matching sewing cotton
Steam iron, pins

1 Cut enough strips of fabric to stretch all around your quilt plus about 15in (40cm) for joining the strips and for turning corners. Cut strips four times the finished width of the binding. The bindings for most of the quilts in this book are ¾in (2cm) wide, so the strips are cut 3in (8cm) wide. Cut off ends of the strips at a 45° angle and join them diagonally, right sides together (*see Fig. A*). On the wrong side of the strip, draw a line down the middle, turn in raw edges up to the line, and press with a steam iron (*see Fig. B*).

2 Thread the needle to match the binding, and the bobbin to match the quilt top. From the back of the quilt, start sewing on the binding halfway along one side leaving about 3in (8cm) free. Sew on pressed line with the binding raw edge in line with the edge of the quilt.

3 At the corners, fold the binding diagonally outward at 45°. Press fold with your finger and mark fold line with a pin (*see Fig. C*). Sew right up to pin, then backstitch a few stitches, raise the needle and pull the threads out a bit without cutting.

4 Remove pin and fold binding outward again on same fold line (*see Fig. D*). Turn the quilt and fold binding back inward so that the new fold is even with the quilt edge. Start sewing again on pressed line, right from quilt edge (*see Fig. E*) Repeat for all four corners.

5 When you reach the starting point, turn in the end of the first raw edge. Cut off excess binding, leaving 2in (5cm) overlap and lay new raw edge on top (*see Fig. F*). Continue sewing until binding has been attached all around.

6 To sew the binding to the front, rewind the bobbin with thread to match binding. Turn quilt right side up and fold binding over so that the folded edge meets the stitching line. Sew with tiny zig-zag stitches overlapping folded edge (*see Fig. G*).

7 When you get to the corners turn quilt and fold binding to form a mitre (*see Fig. H*). Pin folded corner in place as you sew. If you prefer, you can hand-sew binding into place with blind-stitch.

FINISHING CUSHIONS

Making a cushion back is easy and adding a zip makes the cushion easy to remove (see below). You can also add a professional finish by edging cushions with piping. To cover the piping cord, use a similar weight fabric to that of the cushion cover. Strips to make the piping can be cut from the cushion back fabric, or you can use one of the patchwork front fabrics. As a general guide, ½yd (0.5m) of 45in (115cm) wide fabric is enough for two cushion backs and piping for two 15in (38cm) square cushions.

You can buy piping cord by the yard or metre in fabric shops in several widths, but the No.4 size (which is ³⁄₁₆in [4mm] in diameter) is ideal for cushion making.

It is easiest to use your quilter's ruler and rotary cutter (see pp. 10–11) to cut the strips for encasing the piping cord; 1¼in (3.5cm) is the correct width for No.4 cord. You do not have to cut the strips on the bias unless your item has lots of curves. You need to use the zip foot attachment on your sewing machine to encase the piping and to sew it to the cushion.

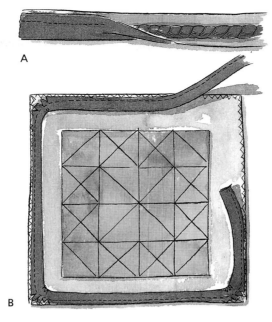

A

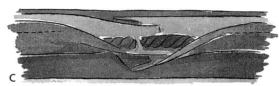

B

C

MATERIALS
No.4 piping cord to go round cushion
Matching fabric strips
Quilter's ruler, rotary cutter (see pp. 10–11), cutting mat
Sewing machine with zip foot attachment
Matching sewing cotton
Finished cushion

that the top is 1in (2.5cm) larger than the finished cushion size. Zig-zag around raw edges. Place one end of encased piping about halfway along side of the cushion top, lining up raw edges (see Fig. B). Leaving about first 2in (5cm) unsewn, stitch close to the piping.

3 Stop sewing 1in (2.5cm) from the first corner and backstitch about 1in (2.5cm). Clip piping in several places where it will bend around the corner, right up to the stitching line of the casing. Continue to sew, rounding off corners. When you are nearing the beginning again, stop sewing and cut casing to overlap the other end by about 1in (2.5cm) and the piping so that it meets other end (see Fig. C). Finish sewing.

SEWING ON PIPING

1 Cut the No.4 piping cord to go around your cushion, plus an extra 2in (5cm). Cut strips of fabric 1¼in (3.5cm) wide and long enough to go around your

cushion, plus about 5in (12cm) for seams. Cut off ends of strips at a 45° angle and join right sides together (see Fig. A on opposite page). Press seams open. Enclose the piping cord inside the piping strip, and sew with a fairly long

stitch (see Fig. A), using a zip foot so that you can sew close to the cord inside the casing.

2 Prepare the completed cushion top (and wadding if quilted) by trimming raw edges so

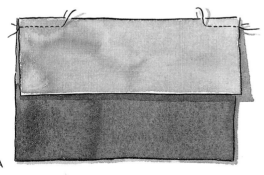

A

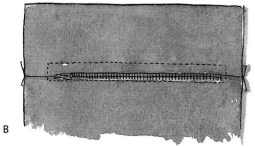

B

INSERTING A ZIP AND SEWING ON BACK

MATERIALS
Steam iron
1 zip, two-thirds of cushion width, pins, sewing machine
Fabric rectangle for cushion back (to size of finished cushion plus 1in [2.5cm] width and 2in [5cm] length)
Matching sewing cotton, cushion pad

1 To insert a zip, fold over one-third of fabric, right sides together (see Fig. A). Press. Sew a ½in (1.3cm) seam with gap for zip. Slit fold; press open. Place zip

under opening with lower fold level with teeth and pin. With zip foot, stitch close to fold along zip length and across zip end. Turn and sew other side ⅜in (9mm) from fold, then across puller end (see Fig. B).

2 To sew on a cushion back, open zip, and pin the back to the front, right sides together. If unpiped, sew with ½in (1.3cm) seam, rounding off corners. Clip the seam allowance at the corners up to the stitching line, trim wadding, and then turn out. Press the cushion back and insert cushion pad. If piped, make as above, sewing with zip foot on piping stitching line.

QUILTS

FOUR-PATCH QUILT

This single quilt proves that you don't need a complicated pattern to make an impressive cover for your bed. The patchwork top, which consists of simple 9in (23cm) blocks, can be sewn in less than a day. It is created with the "slice and dice" method, which involves cutting strips, sewing them together, then cutting across the sewn pieces. If you tie the quilt together instead of quilting it around each block, you could be sleeping under it tonight! The four-patch blocks look most effective if two of the diagonally opposite prints are slightly darker than the other two. The fabrics specified are all 45in (115cm) wide unless otherwise stated.

MATERIALS

finished size: 63in x 99in (158cm x 249cm)

¾yd (0.7m) each of four pastel floral-print cotton fabrics (A, B, C and D) for the four-patch blocks

3⅜yd (3.1m) of pink floral print fabric for the large blocks and binding

5½yd (5m) of 36in (90cm) or 45in (115cm) wide, or 2¾yd (2.5m) of 94in (1.9m) wide, toning cotton sheeting for back

64in x 100in (1.65m x 2.6m) piece of 2oz (50g) polyester wadding

Rotary cutter (see pp. 10–11)

Quilter's ruler

Cutting mat

Matching sewing cotton

Steam iron

Long needle

Stranded embroidery cotton

Scissors

1 "Slice" each piece of the floral print fabrics A, B, C and D into five strips 5in (13cm) wide and about 44in (1.2m) long. With the strips rights side together, sew with ¼in (6mm) seams (see p. 9) to make pairs of A/B and C/D (see Fig. A). Press seams toward A or C with a steam iron.

2 "Dice" each strip-pair into pieces 5in (13cm) wide, as shown in Fig A.

3 Sew an A/B piece to D/C piece, matching up the seams, as shown in Fig. B. Repeat to make 39 four-patch blocks, each measuring 9½in (25cm) square. Press the blocks.

4 Slice the pink floral print fabric for the large squares into ten strips 9½in (25cm) wide (save some material for binding). Dice each strip to make four 9½in (25cm) squares. You need a total of 38 squares in all.

5 Sew the four-patch blocks and the large squares together to make 11 rows, alternating them as shown in the photograph. Press the seams of all the four-patch blocks outward. Sew all the rows together, matching up the seams. Press the patchwork.

6 Join the sheeting fabric for the back, if necessary, and then make your "quilt sandwich" (see pp. 18–19). To tie your quilt, thread a long needle with three strands of embroidery cotton and take a stitch through all three layers at the corners and also in the middle of each block. Cut the embroidery cotton so that the ends are about 2in (5cm) long. Tie these ends firmly with a double knot and then trim with scissors.

7 Cut seven strips 3in (8cm) wide across the width of the pink floral-print fabric for the binding and sew as described in Binding a Quilt (see p. 20).

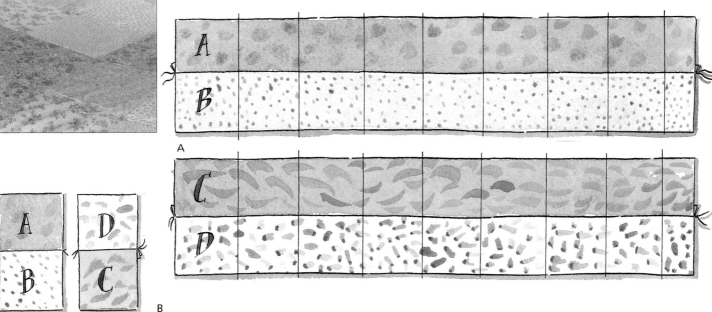

A

B

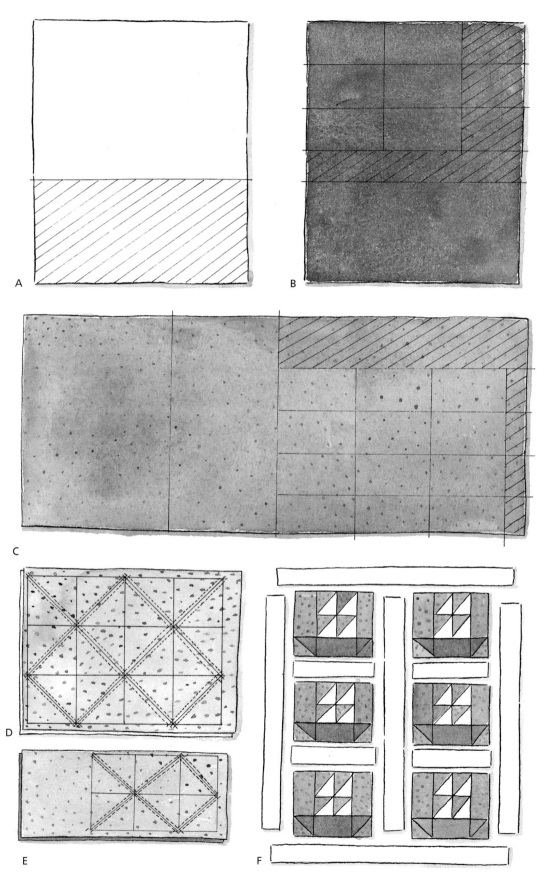

A

B

C

D

E

F

MATERIALS

finished size: 29in x 34in (73.5cm x 86cm)

½yd (0.45m) of mid-blue print cotton fabric

1 fat quarter (*see p. 8*) each of white and dark-blue cotton fabrics

⅓yd (0.3m) of white cotton fabric for sashing and borders

⅓yd (0.3m) of dark-blue cotton fabric for binding and straps

1yd (0.9m) of towelling

1yd (0.9m) of 4oz (100g) polyester wadding

No.2 template from 3inch-set of R.I.T. Squares (*see pp. 108–109*)

Ballpoint or fine felt-tip pen

Rotary cutter (*see pp.10–11*)

Quilter's ruler, cutting mat

Matching sewing cotton

Steam iron

1 For six boats, you need 24 No.2 R.I.T. Square sails. From the mid-blue print fabric and the fat quarter of white fabric cut pieces 13in x 18in (33cm x 46cm) as in Figs. A and C. Press pieces right sides together and use No.2 R.I.T. Square template to draw a grid of 12 squares (*see Fig. D*). Sew and cut (*see pp.12–13*). All seams are ¼in (6mm) unless otherwise stated. Press seams toward darker side with a steam iron.

2 From mid-blue print fabric and the fat quarter of dark-blue fabric cut pieces 9in x 18in (23cm x 46cm) as in Figs. B and C. Draw, sew and cut six No.2 R.I.T. Squares as in Step 1 to make six bows and six sterns (*see Fig. E*).

3 From remaining piece of dark-blue fabric cut three strips 3½in (9cm) wide. From each strip cut two pieces 6½in (16.5cm) long for the boats (*see Fig. B*). From remaining mid-blue print fabric, cut four strips 3½in (9cm) wide and 22in (56cm) long. From each strip cut three 6½in (16.5cm) lengths for the sky (see Fig. C).

4 Join the sails to make a pair for each mast. Sew together the sky patches and the sails, and sew the bow and stern to each boat. Press seams toward the darker side. Join the sail portion to the boat portion of each block, matching seams. Press the blocks.

5 From the white fabric for sashing, cut five long strips 2¼in (5.75cm) wide. From the ends of four strips cut four pieces 12½in (32cm) long and sew them between blocks (see Fig. F). Press seams toward sashing. Cut three strips to same length as the columns of boats and sew to each side of the columns (see Fig. F). Press seams toward the sashing.

6 Cut two strips to length of patchwork width and sew to top and bottom. Press seams toward the borders. Cut a strip 3in x 44in (7.5cm x 112cm) long from dark-blue fabric for straps. Fold in half lengthways, then fold edges into foldline. Stitch close to edge along each side. Cut two straps 18in (46cm) long.

7 Cut towelling pieces and wadding to patchwork size. Pin the wadding to wrong side of towelling. Fold under the ends of the straps and sew to right side of the towelling (see Fig. G). Make a quilt sandwich (see pp. 18–19). Machine quilt using the "stitch-in-the-ditch" method (see p. 17) around each block (avoiding straps at back). From the dark-blue fabric, cut four 2in (5cm) wide strips for a narrow ½in (1.3cm) binding. Sew on binding (see p. 20), but don't sew over straps. Fig. G shows you how to fold the mat.

EASY LEVEL

BABY CHANGING MAT

This versatile sailing boat changing mat, which has an absorbent towelling back and handy carrying straps, can be folded up to hold everything a baby needs on a day out. The six boat blocks are easy to make in the cotton fabrics, using the R.I.T. Square method (see pp. 12–13). The fabrics specified are all 45in (115cm) wide unless otherwise stated. Be sure to wash them all before you start sewing the mat.

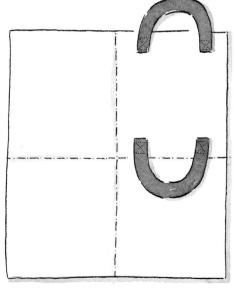

G

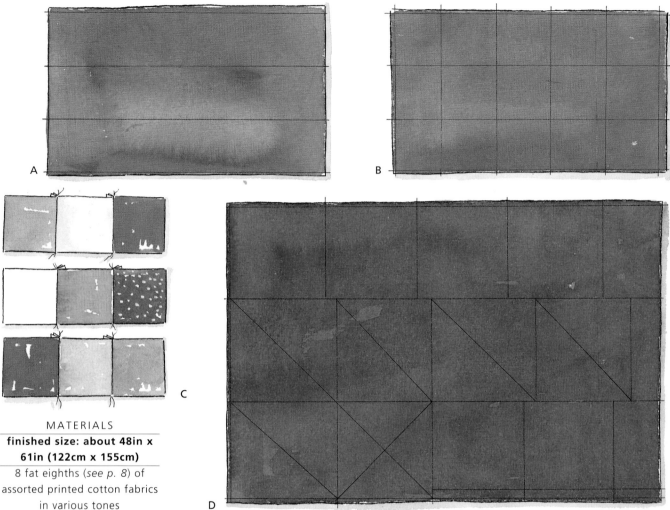

A

B

C

D

MATERIALS

finished size: about 48in x 61in (122cm x 155cm)

8 fat eighths (*see p. 8*) of assorted printed cotton fabrics in various tones

1yd (0.9m) of crimson cotton fabric

¼yd (0.25m) of mauve print cotton fabric for narrow border

¾yd (0.7m) of navy print cotton fabric for wide border

⅝yd (0.6m) of maroon cotton fabric for binding

1¾yd (1.6m) of 60in (150cm) wide, or 3½yd (3.2m) of 45in (115cm) wide, toning cotton backing fabric

1¾yd (1.6m) of 54in (140cm) wide 2oz (50g) polyester wadding

Rotary cutter (*see pp. 10–11*), quilter's ruler, cutting mat, steam iron

Matching sewing cotton

Quilting materials and design (*see pp. 16–17*)

1 Cut eight printed fabric pieces for nine-patch blocks into three long strips, 3½in (9cm) wide (*see Fig. A*). Cut strips into five 3½in (9cm) squares (*see Fig. B*), making 120 3½in (9cm) patches (you only need 108 for 12 blocks). Choose nine dark and light patches and arrange in a block. Sew together with ¼in (6mm) seams (*see Fig. C*). Press seams of alternate rows in opposite direction with steam iron. Sew three rows together, matching seams. Press. Make 12 nine-patch blocks with randomly chosen patches, 9½in (24cm) square.

2 Following Fig. D, cut out plain squares. First cut a strip 9½in (24cm) wide from crimson fabric. Cut strip into four 9½in (24cm)

squares. Next, cut two strips 10½in (27cm) wide. Cut six 10½in (27cm) and two 9½in (24cm) squares. Fold large squares diagonally as shown. Cut on fold lines to make ten big triangles for sides and four small triangles for corners.

3 Arrange blocks and triangles in eight diagonal rows (*see Fig. E*), so darks and lights in blocks are scattered. Sew together in rows. Press seams of blocks outward, stretching rows to lie straight. Then trim fabric from triangles. Sew eight rows together, matching seams. Press and square off edges. From mauve print fabric, cut five strips 1½in (4cm) wide. Join end to end and press seams open. Cut two

strips to patchwork width and sew to top and bottom. Cut two more to patchwork length and sew to each side. Press seams outward.

4 From navy print fabric, cut five strips 4½in (12cm) wide and join as before. Cut two strips to patchwork width and sew to top and bottom. Cut two more to patchwork length and sew to each side. Make "quilt sandwich" with wadding and backing fabric (*see pp. 18–19*), joining backing fabric if necessary. Using quilting design, transfer to the crimson squares and quilt by hand, if preferred (*see pp. 16–17*). Cut six binding strips 3in (8cm) wide from maroon fabric width and sew on (*see p. 20*).

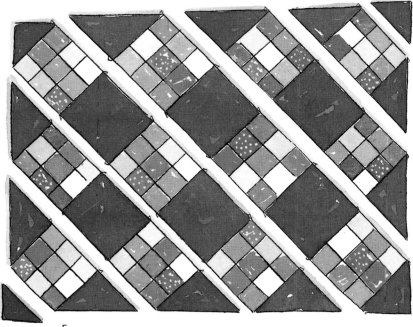

E

NINE-PATCH QUILT

This quilt is very easy to make and helps use up all those pretty bits of material that you have hidden away in the bottom of your scrap bag. The nine-patch blocks are made up of patches that are cut from eight different printed cotton fabrics. You can decorate the large, plain squares that alternate with the nine-patch blocks with an attractive quilting pattern, such as the flower design shown on page 16. But if you prefer not to quilt, just use a printed fabric instead. The fabrics specified are 45in (115cm) wide unless otherwise stated.

MATERIALS

**finished size: about 49in x
58in (124cm x 148cm)**

1yd (1m) of white cotton
background fabric

8 fat eighths (*see p.8*) of
assorted dark- to mid-green
print cotton fabrics

½yd (0.5m) of mid-green
cotton fabric for narrow
framing

1⅛yd (1.05m) of pale-green
cotton fabric for sashing and
wide border

1⅔yd (1.5m) of 60in (150cm)
wide toning backing fabric

1⅔yd (1.5m) of 54in (140cm)
wide 2oz (50g) polyester
wadding

⅝yd (0.6m) of dark-green print
cotton fabric for binding

No.2 template from the 3-inch
set of R.I.T. Squares
(*see pp. 108–109*)

Ballpoint or fine felt-tip pen

Rotary cutter (*see pp. 10–11*)

Quilter's ruler, cutting mat

Matching sewing cotton

Steam iron

Quilting materials (optional)
and design (*see pp. 16–17*)

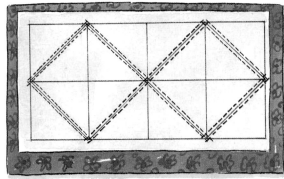

A

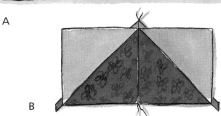

B

1 First make the geese as
follows. From the white cotton
fabric cut eight pieces about 8½in
x 16½in (22cm x 42cm). Place one
of the pieces right sides together
with one of the green print
fabrics. Use the No.2 R.I.T. Square
template as a guide to draw a grid
of eight squares (*see Fig. A*). Sew
and cut (*see pp. 12–13*) to make
16 No. 2 patches. All seams are
¼in (6mm). Press the seams
toward the light colour with a
steam iron.

2 Sew the patches together to
make 8 geese (*see Fig. B*).
Press the seams open. Repeat with
the remaining seven green print
fabrics to make 64 geese.

3 Arrange the 64 geese on the
floor randomly into four rows
of 16 geese as shown in the
photograph. Place two "twin"
geese in each row. This step takes
quite a long time because you
have to check that no twins are
adjacent and that there is a nice
balance of the prints overall. Sew
up the four rows of geese,
matching the vertical seams. Clip
off the points at the top and press
seams downward. Use the steam
iron to block the rows by
stretching or easing the geese in
each row to fit along a straight
line drawn on your ironing board.

4 Now make the narrow
framing. From the mid-green
fabric cut 11 strips 1½in (4cm)
wide and about 44in (115cm)
long. Sew nine strips together end
to end, press the seams open, and
divide them into eight pieces of
equal length. Cut all pieces to the
exact length of a row of geese
and sew them to each side of
each row keeping the rows
straight. Press seams outward.

5 From the pale-green fabric,
cut four strips 3½in (9cm)
wide and about 44in (115cm)

long. Sew them end to end and
press the seams open. Cut three
strips exactly the length of a row
of geese and sew one between
each row. Press the seams toward
the narrow framing. Cut the
remaining two mid-green framing
strips to the exact width of the
patchwork and sew to top and
bottom. Press the seams outward.

6 Make the wide border next.
From the pale-green fabric cut
5 strips 4½in (11.5cm) wide and
about 44in (115cm) long. Cut two
strips exactly the width of the
patchwork and sew to top and
bottom. Press seams toward the
narrow framing. Sew the
remaining three strips together,
end to end. Cut two strips exactly
the length of the patchwork and
sew one to each side. Press seams
inward and press the whole quilt.

7 Make your "quilt sandwich"
with the wadding and
backing fabric (*see pp. 18–19*).
Quilt by hand or machine around
the geese and on each side of
each strip, using the "stitch-in-
the-ditch" method (*see p. 17*). If
you wish to add decorative
quilting on the border and

sashing, transfer the quilting
design with the "prick-and-
pounce" method (*see pp. 16–17*),
and go over the lines with a quilt
marker. Quilt along the marked
lines. Cut six strips 3in (7.5cm)
wide across the width of the dark-
green print fabric for the binding
and then sew on as described in
the Binding a Quilt section on
page 20.

EASY LEVEL

FLYING GEESE THROW

The "Flying Geese" pattern used for this throw, which is ideal to put on a bed or sofa, is a traditional American patchwork design. Whereas many American designs, such as "Jacob's Ladder" (*see pp. 34–35*), are made up by repeating the same block, the Flying Geese pattern comes into the category of a strip quilt. Instead of using a block arrangement, the geese are placed together in long columns which are then separated by sashing. The border and sashing in this project are finished with decorative quilting which you can either stitch by hand or by machine. All the fabrics specified are 45in (115cm) wide unless otherwise stated.

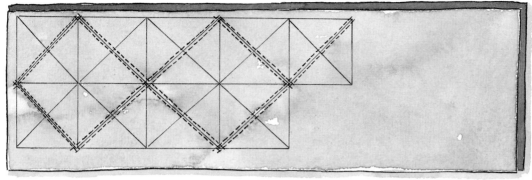

A

B

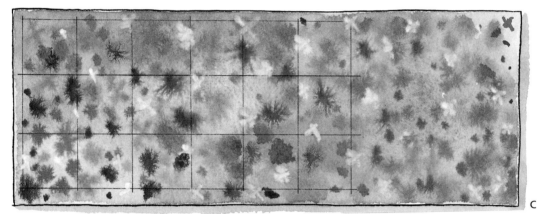

C

MATERIALS

finished size: about 37in x 47in (94cm x 120cm)

⅜yd (0.35m) each of coral and dark-pink cotton fabrics for R.I.T. Squares

½yd (0.5m) of bold, floral print cotton fabric for large squares

¼yd (0.25m) each of dark-green, white and printed cotton fabrics for three narrow borders

1fat quarter (*see p. 8*) each of bright-green and dark-pink cotton fabrics for striped border

½yd (0.5m) of print cotton fabric for wide border

1⅓yd (1.3m) of matching backing fabric

1⅓yd (1.3m) of 2oz (50g) polyester wadding

½yd (0.5m) of dark-green cotton fabric for binding

Steam iron, ballpoint pen, rotary cutter (*see pp. 10–11*), quilter's ruler, cutting mat, matching sewing cotton

LIBERTY SQUARES WALL HANGING

This quilt was designed as a stunning wall hanging, but by just adding some more blocks you can easily adapt it to make a bed quilt. The large squares are cut from an eye-catching bold floral print and are then alternated with blocks that are created with the R.I.T. Square method (*see pp. 12–13*). One of the features of this quilt is its interesting border. You can add as many bands of fabric as you want, omitting the striped border for a really quick design. The fabrics specified for the quilt are all 45in (115cm) wide unless otherwise stated.

D

1 Using the R.I.T. Square method make 17 patches. Press coral and dark-pink cotton fabrics right sides together with steam iron. Draw grid of nine squares 6in x 6in (15cm x 15cm) with diagonal lines through corners (*see Fig. A*). Sew and cut (*see pp. 12–13*) 36 half-patches with ¼in (6mm) seams. Open out and press seams toward dark-pink side. Sort half-patches into two mirror-image rows (*see Fig. B*). Sew together by pairs in a kite string of 18 R.I.T. Square patches (discard one). Press seams to one side – patches should be 5¼in (13.5cm) square. From floral print, cut six strips 5¼in (13.5cm) wide and 18in (50cm) long. From each strip cut three 5¼in (13.5cm) squares (18) (*see Fig. C*). Sew R.I.T. Square patches and plain squares together alternately to make seven rows (*see picture*). Press alternate rows' seams in opposite directions.

Sew seven rows together, matching seams. Press well.

2 For first narrow border, cut strips 1½in (3.5cm) wide from print fabric. Join strips to extend around patchwork. Sew on strips (mitre corners on a border print). For second border, cut four strips 1¼in (3cm) wide from dark-green fabric. Cut two to patchwork length, sew to side edges and press seams outward. Cut other two to its width. Sew to top and bottom and press seams outward. For third border, cut strips 1in (2.5cm) wide from white fabric and sew as above.

3 Make striped border. Press two fat quarters right sides together, then cut 11 strips 22in (56cm) long and 1½in (3.5cm) wide. Sew two colours together in pairs and sew strip-pairs together in a "strippy" sheet 22in x 22in (56cm x 56cm) square (see Fig. D). Press seams in same direction. Cut across stripes for 8 striped strips 2in (5cm) wide (see Fig. D). Join to make four, long striped strips.

4 Cut two striped strips to patchwork length, and other two to its width. (Cut symmetrically with same colour at each end.) Cut four 2in (5cm) squares from floral print. Sew two to shorter strips' ends. Sew two longer strips to each patchwork side, pressing seams inward. Sew shorter strips to top and bottom, matching corner seams; press inward. For final border, cut five strips from print fabric, 3½in (9cm) wide. Join strips end to end. Cut strips to length and sew as Step 2. With wadding and backing fabric make "quilt sandwich" (see pp. 18–19). Work machine quilting with "stitch-in-the-ditch" method (see p. 17). Cut four binding strips 3in (8cm) wide across width of dark-green fabric and sew on (see p. 20).

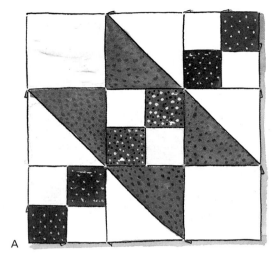

A

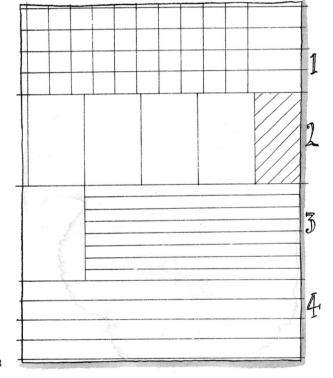

B

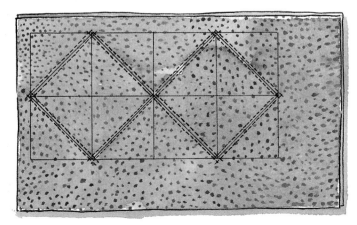

C

MATERIALS

finished size: about 41in x 50in (104cm x 127cm)

1⅝yd (1.5m) of white cotton fabric for background

3 fat eighths (*see p. 8*) of assorted navy print cotton fabrics

5 fat eighths of assorted mid-tone print cotton fabrics

⅓yd (0.3m) each of navy print and light print cotton fabric for second and third border

1½yd (1.4m) of toning backing fabric

1⅓yd (1.2m) of 54in (140cm) wide 2oz (50g) polyester wadding

⅜yd (0.35m) of maroon cotton fabric for binding

No.1 and No.2 templates from the 3-inch set of R.I.T. Squares (*see pp. 108–109*)

Ballpoint or fine felt-tip pen

Rotary cutter (*see pp. 10–11*)

Quilter's ruler

Cutting mat

Matching sewing cotton

Steam iron

Quilting materials and design (*see pp. 16–17*)

1 The quilt is made up of 20 nine-patch blocks (*see Fig. A*) using the R.I.T. Square method. Each block has two No.1 patches (plain squares); make these 40 patches first. Using a rotary cutter,

D

cut four strips 3½in (9cm) wide from white cotton background fabric, then cut ten 3½in (9cm) squares from each strip (*see Fig. B1*). If you don't have a rotary cutter, use the No.1 R.I.T. Square template to trace patches and cut out with scissors.

2 From the white background material cut five pieces about 9in x 16in (23cm x 41cm) (*see Fig B2*). Press one of white pieces right sides together with one of the mid-toned fabrics. Use the No.2 R.I.T. Square template to draw a grid (*see Fig. C*). Sew and cut (*see pp. 12–13*) to make 16 No. 2 patches. All seams are ¼in (6mm).

3 Repeat Step 2 with four other mid-toned print fabrics to make 80 No.2 patches. Now make checkerboard patches for the "ladders". From the white fabric cut eight strips 2in (5cm) wide and 36in (90cm) long (*see Fig B3*). Cut in half to make 16 strips about 18in (45cm) long. From each navy-print fabric cut five strips 2in (5cm) wide and about 18in (45cm) long. One white strip is left.

4 With right sides together, sew each white strip to a navy print strip along their lengths and press seams toward the darker side. Cut each strip-set into eight pieces 2in (5cm) wide. Choosing the three navy prints randomly, turn alternate pieces upside down and sew together in pairs, matching seams, to make 60 3½in (9cm) square patches (*see Fig. D*). Clip seam at back and press each half toward darker side.

5 Now assemble blocks. Sew patches together (*see Fig. A*). The four No.2 patches should be the same, but the checkerboard patches should be placed so that there is a scattering of the navy

prints in each block. Press seams away from the No.2 patches. Sew three rows for each block together; line up seams carefully. Press with steam iron. Place blocks on floor so that all checkerboard "ladders" are ascending in the same direction. Arrange blocks so that no identical ones are adjacent. Sew blocks together to make five rows, then sew rows together. Press well.

6 For first border, cut four strips from white fabric measuring 2½in (5cm) wide and about 45in (115cm) long (*see Fig. B4*). Join together end to end. From this length, cut two strips to patchwork width and sew to top and bottom. Cut two more strips to patchwork length and sew to either side. Press seams outward. For second border,

cut five strips 1½in (4cm) wide and same length as first, from navy print, join and sew as Step 6. For final border, cut five strips 2in (5cm) wide and same length as first, from light print. Join and sew as Step 6.

7 Make a "quilt sandwich" with the wadding and backing fabric (*see pp. 18–19*). Transfer quilting design on pages 16–17 onto the No.1 patches so that the hearts' bases meet at the checkerboard patches' corners. Quilt by hand or machine. The remainder of the quilt can be quilted by machine using the "stitch-in-the-ditch" method (*see p. 17*) around all the squares, triangles and borders. Then, cut out five 3in (8cm) strips across the width of the maroon fabric for the binding and sew as described on page 20.

JACOB'S LADDER COT QUILT

The natural-coloured cotton fabrics used in this cot quilt make a welcome change from the pastel or primary shades which are the usual favourites in a child's nursery. The "Jacob's Ladder" pattern is a traditional American nine-patch block design. Non-symmetrical blocks like these look best repeated in a quilt rather than used alone in a cushion or sampler, because the little squares and triangles join up to create interesting diagonals in two directions. The design is straightforward to make using the R.I.T. Square method (*see pp. 12–13*). The fabrics specified are all 45in (115cm) wide unless otherwise stated.

TRIP-AROUND-THE-WORLD THROW

The fascinating pattern displayed on this quilt is "Trip around the World" – a traditional Amish design. While the Amish always used plain fabrics in rich, jewel-like colours, the quilt in the photograph is made with a most unusual print fabric that is reminiscent of natural textures in bright sapphire shades. You could, however, use any interesting cotton fabrics as long as they range in tone from light to dark. You will need seven different tones for this quilt. Unless otherwise specified, the fabrics are 45in (115cm) wide.

Typically, the Trip-around-the-World design is always square. Imagine how time-consuming it would be to cut out and sew together individually all the 529 little squares that are included in this quilt! Fortunately for you, making this large throw is as easy as cutting strips with your rotary cutter, sewing them together and then "dicing" across them to produce the necessary rows of different-coloured squares.

MATERIALS

finished size: about 54in x 54in (137cm x 137cm)

1 fat quarter (*see p. 8*) each of a very light-blue and a very dark-blue print cotton fabric

½yd (0.5m) each of five other blue print cotton fabrics, ranging from dark to light blue

1yd (1m) of blue striped cotton fabric for border

¼yd (0.25m) of dark-blue cotton fabric for corners

1½yd (1.4m) of 60in (150cm) wide, or 3yd (2.7m) of 45in (115cm) wide, toning backing fabric

1½yd (1.4m) of 54in (140cm) wide 2oz (50g) polyester wadding

½yd (0.5m) of navy cotton fabric for binding

Rotary cutter (*see pp. 10–11*)

Quilter's ruler

Cutting mat

Seven small plastic bags labelled 1 to 7

Matching sewing cotton

Seam unpicker

Steam iron

Invisible nylon thread for machine quilting

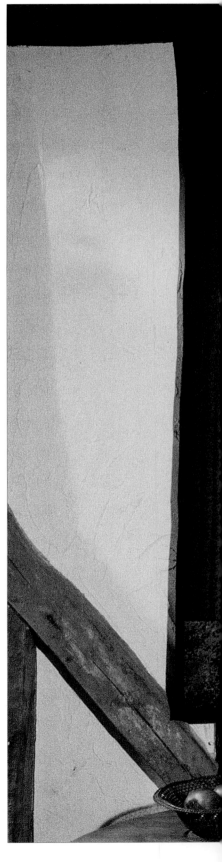

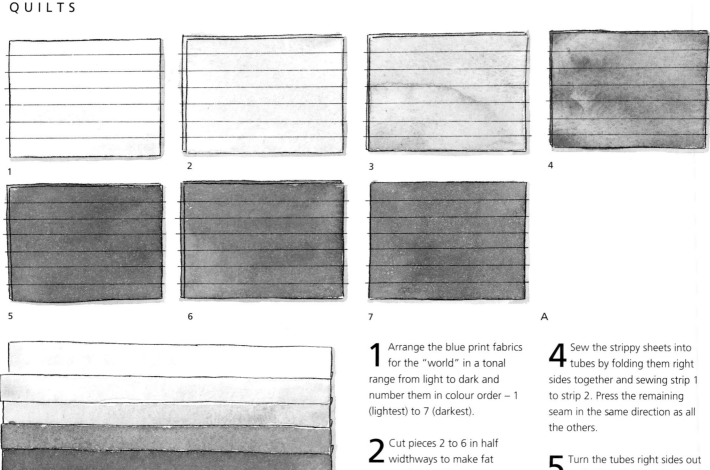

1

2

3

4

5

6

7

A

B

C

1 Arrange the blue print fabrics for the "world" in a tonal range from light to dark and number them in colour order – 1 (lightest) to 7 (darkest).

2 Cut pieces 2 to 6 in half widthways to make fat quarters (*see p. 8*). Use your rotary cutter to "slice" strips 2¼in (6cm) wide and about 22in (56cm) long. You will get seven strips from the pieces numbered 1 and 7 and 14 strips from pieces 2 to 6 (*see Fig. A*). Place all the different strips of fabric in the appropriate numbered plastic bags.

3 Sew all the fabric strips together with ¼in (6mm) seams to make seven "strippy sheets" in this order: 1 – 2 – 3 – 4 – 5 – 6 – 7 – 6 – 5 – 4 – 3 – 2 (*see Fig. B*) and then press all the seams with a steam iron, making sure you iron them all in the same direction. When you are sewing, be careful not to stretch any of the strips, otherwise the sheets will not lie straight. Always start sewing from the same end and keep the ends even on one side (not all the strips will be exactly the same length).

4 Sew the strippy sheets into tubes by folding them right sides together and sewing strip 1 to strip 2. Press the remaining seam in the same direction as all the others.

5 Turn the tubes right sides out and "dice" them with your rotary cutter in little rings 2¼in (6cm) wide (*see Fig. C*). Be careful to cut the rings exactly at right angles to the strips of the tubes. You can dice seven or eight rings from each tube, and you need 46 rings in total. Keep any leftover fabric in the numbered bags to help you keep track of the various fabrics later.

6 Now begin to organize the first pieces for the "eastern hemisphere" of the world. For Row 1, take a ring and hold it right side toward you with the seams toward the right; unpick it between Pieces 2 and 3. Turn the ring for Row 2 the other way round so that its seams go toward the left; unpick it between Pieces 3 and 4. Lay the pieces as in the chart on page 39. For each row, refer to the diagram, and unpick between the patch number in the

Eastern hemisphere chart:

3	4	5	6	7	6	5	4	3	2	1	2	ROW 1
4	5	6	7	6	5	4	3	2	1	2	3	ROW 2
5	6	7	6	5	4	3	2	1	2	3	4	ROW 3
6	7	6	5	4	3	2	1	2	3	4	5	ROW 4
7	6	5	4	3	2	1	2	3	4	5	6	ROW 5
6	5	4	3	2	1	2	3	4	5	6	7	ROW 6
5	4	3	2	1	2	3	4	5	6	7	6	ROW 7
4	3	2	1	2	3	4	5	6	7	6	5	ROW 8
3	2	1	2	3	4	5	6	7	6	5	4	ROW 9
2	1	2	3	4	5	6	7	6	5	4	3	ROW 10
1	2	3	4	5	6	7	6	5	4	3	2	ROW 11
2	3	4	5	6	7	6	5	4	3	2	1	ROW 12
1	2	3	4	5	6	7	6	5	4	3	2	ROW 13
2	1	2	3	4	5	6	7	6	5	4	3	ROW 14
3	2	1	2	3	4	5	6	7	6	5	4	ROW 15
4	3	2	1	2	3	4	5	6	7	6	5	ROW 16
5	4	3	2	1	2	3	4	5	6	7	6	ROW 17
6	5	4	3	2	1	2	3	4	5	6	7	ROW 18
7	6	5	4	3	2	1	2	3	4	5	6	ROW 19
6	7	6	5	4	3	2	1	2	3	4	5	ROW 20
5	6	7	6	5	4	3	2	1	2	3	4	ROW 21
4	5	6	7	6	5	4	3	2	1	2	3	ROW 22
3	4	5	6	7	6	5	4	3	2	1	2	ROW 23

Western hemisphere chart:

2	1	2	3	4	5	6	7	6	5	4	3
3	2	1	2	3	4	5	6	7	6	5	4
4	3	2	1	2	3	4	5	6	7	6	5
5	4	3	2	1	2	3	4	5	6	7	6
6	5	4	3	2	1	2	3	4	5	6	7
7	6	5	4	3	2	1	2	3	4	5	6
6	7	6	5	4	3	2	1	2	3	4	5
5	6	7	6	5	4	3	2	1	2	3	4
4	5	6	7	6	5	4	3	2	1	2	3
3	4	5	6	7	6	5	4	3	2	1	2
2	3	4	5	6	7	6	5	4	3	2	1
1*	2	3	4	5	6	7	6	5	4	3	2
2	3	4	5	6	7	6	5	4	3	2	1
3	4	5	6	7	6	5	4	3	2	1	2
4	5	6	7	6	5	4	3	2	1	2	3
5	6	7	6	5	4	3	2	1	2	3	4
6	7	6	5	4	3	2	1	2	3	4	5
7	6	5	4	3	2	1	2	3	4	5	6
6	5	4	3	2	1	2	3	4	5	6	7
5	4	3	2	1	2	3	4	5	6	7	6
4	3	2	1	2	3	4	5	6	7	6	5
3	2	1	2	3	4	5	6	7	6	5	4
2	1	2	3	4	5	6	7	6	5	4	3

left-hand column and the patch number in the right-hand column. Check the numbered bags to make sure you are unpicking the right colour! The seams of the odd-numbered rows go toward the right and those of the even-numbered rows go toward the left. As the pattern of the eastern hemisphere starts to form, sew the rows together, matching the seams carefully.

7 When you get to Row 12, unpick between Pieces 1 and 2, but unpick and discard Piece 1 (starred on the chart) and replace it with a little square cut from one of the dark-coloured fabrics.

Continue sewing carefully following the numbered diagram exactly, until you have sewn together the 23 rows of the eastern hemisphere.

8 For the "western hemisphere", follow the instructions as for Step 6. However, reverse the colours of the rings and, for each row, unpick and discard the patch in the highlighted column in the chart. Sew together the 23 rows with seams of alternate rows going in opposite directions.

9 Press all the horizontal seams of the eastern hemisphere upward and those of the western

hemisphere downward. Sew the two hemispheres together, being careful to match the seams. Press the world carefully.

10 Cut four strips 8in (20cm) wide from the blue-striped fabric for the border. (The width of the border can vary depending on the width of the stripes.) Cut the four strips to exactly the same length as the sides of the world. Then cut four dark-blue squares to match the width of the border strips. Sew two of the border strips to the opposite sides of the world. Sew the dark-blue squares to each end of the other two border strips and sew these to the

remaining two sides of the world, taking care to match up the seams neatly. Press the seams toward the border strips.

11 To finish, make your "quilt sandwich" with the wadding and backing fabric (see pp. 18–19), joining the backing fabric if necessary. Machine quilt diagonally across the small squares using invisible nylon thread and around the borders using the "stitch-in-the-ditch" method (see p. 17). Cut six strips 3in (8cm) wide across the width of the navy fabric for the binding and then sew onto the throw as fully described on p. 20.

MATERIALS

finished size: about 37in x 44in (94cm x 112cm)
¾yd (0.7m) of dark-green print cotton fabric for stars
1 fat quarter (*see p. 8*) of brown print cotton fabric
5 9in (24cm) square scraps of very light print cotton fabric
1 fat quarter of large floral print cotton fabric
6 fat quarters in brown and brick-red cotton fabrics, or fabric scraps about 22in (55cm) long for 56 strips 1¾in (4.5cm) wide
¼yd (0.25m) of dark-green print cotton fabric for first border
½yd (0.3m) of very light print cotton fabric for second border plus small brown print cotton scrap for corners
1⅛yd (1m) of toning backing fabric
1⅛yd (1m) of 54in (140cm) wide 2oz (50g) polyester wadding
⅜yd (0.35m) of plain dark-green cotton fabric for binding
No.2 template from the 3-inch set of R.I.T. Squares (*see pp. 108–109*)
White marking pencil and ballpoint pen
Rotary cutter (*see pp. 10–11*)
Quilter's ruler
Cutting mat
Steam iron
Matching sewing cotton

WALLED GARDEN HANGING

This beautiful wall hanging in softly coloured floral prints makes an eye-catching feature in any living room. It is based on a block pattern called "Ohio Star" and is a scrap quilt in the true sense of the word. You can use as many suitable cotton fabrics as you like – bits left over from dressmaking and jumble sale bargains are ideal. Try to find fabrics that are of a similar weight, and remember to wash all scrap fabrics first to make sure they don't shrink or run. The "Walled Garden" design only really works successfully if you organize the fabrics so that the darkest tone forms the points of the star in the nine-patch block and the lightest tone creates the little diamonds. Consider the overall colour carefully, too.

In the hanging in the photograph, dark-green stars are complemented by rich brick reds and browns. Choose a pretty floral print for the patches in the middle of the blocks. The fabrics specified for the hanging are all 45in (115cm) wide unless otherwise stated.

The Walled Garden hanging is made by the R.I.T. Square method (*see pp. 12–13*), using the 3-inch set. By using a No.2 template (which is slightly smaller than a No.3 template) to make a No.3 patch, the size of the hanging is scaled down to create a more intricate-looking design.

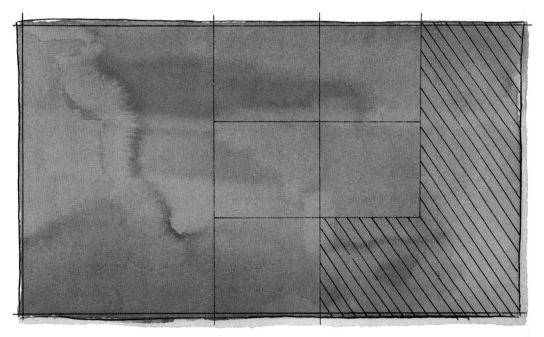

A

1 First make the points of the stars. From the dark-green fabric cut a piece 18in x 27in (46cm x 70cm) (*see Fig. A*). Place it right sides together with the brown print fabric. With a marking pencil draw a grid of 20 squares (*see Fig. B*). (Note that for this design you are using the No.2 R.I.T. Square template for No.3 patches rather than the No.3 template.)

Sew and cut 80 half-patches with ¼in (6mm) seams (*see p.12*). Press seams with a steam iron toward the darker side.

2 From the dark-green print fabric cut five 9in (23cm) squares (*see Fig. A*). Place one piece right sides together with one of the very light print fabric squares. Draw a grid of four

squares using the No.2 R.I.T. Square template as a guide (*see Fig. C*). Sew and cut 16 half-patches. Press seams toward darker side. Repeat with other four light print fabric squares to make 80 half-patches.

3 To complete the stars' points, sew together half-patches from Step 1 and Step 2 so that the brown print and light print are

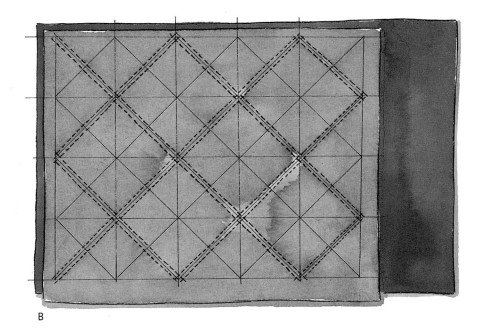

B

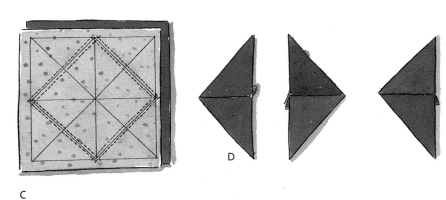

C

D

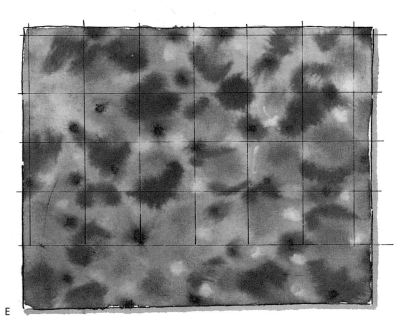

E

always opposite (*see Fig. D*). Press seams to one side.

4 Now make middle square of each block. From floral print cut four strips 3⅛in (8cm) wide and 22in (56cm) long (*see Fig. E*). From each strip cut five 3⅛in (8cm) squares.

5 Next make "strippy" sheets from brown and red fat quarters or scraps to cut corner squares. Cut 56 strips about 22in (60cm) long, 1¾in (4.5cm) wide. Sew 14 strips together randomly for a strippy sheet about 22in x 19in (60cm x 50cm). Make three more strippy sheets and press seams to one side. "Block" sheets (*see p. 18*) so that strips are straight.

6 From each strippy sheet cut diagonal strips 3⅛in (8cm) wide (*see Fig. F*). From each strip cut 3⅛in (8cm) squares, making sure that a seam runs from corner to corner on each square – you need 80.

7 Next, assemble blocks. Choose a patch with a different light print piece for each No.3 patch in each block, and a good mix of scraps for each corner. Sew blocks together (*see Fig. G*). First sew three patches to form rows and then sew rows together, matching seams. Make 20 blocks, and press.

8 Lay blocks on floor in five rows of four blocks each. Keep re-arranging to make a good colour balance in the scrap corners. Check that no two identical light prints are adjacent when No.3 patches are together. Sew blocks together, in rows first, then pin rows, matching up seams. Press and block.

9 From the dark-green print for the first border cut four strips 1½in (4cm) wide. Cut two strips to

42

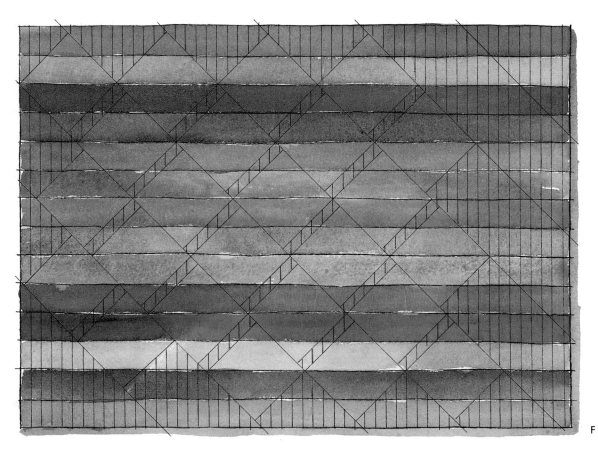

F

patchwork's width and sew to top and bottom. Cut two more strips to its length and sew one to each side. Press seams outward.

10 From light print fabric for the second border cut four strips 2¾in (7cm) wide. Cut two strips to patchwork's width and two to patchwork's length. Cut four 2¾in (7cm) squares from brown print fabric. Sew two to each end of shorter strips. Sew the two longer strips to each patchwork side and press. Sew two shorter strips to top and bottom, matching corner seams.

11 Make your "quilt sandwich" with wadding and backing fabric (*see pp. 18–19*). Quilt by machine around the points of the stars and borders, using the "stitch-in-the-ditch" method (*see p. 17*). Cut four 3in (8cm) strips across dark-green fabric's width for binding and sew on (*see p. 20*).

G

CUSHIONS

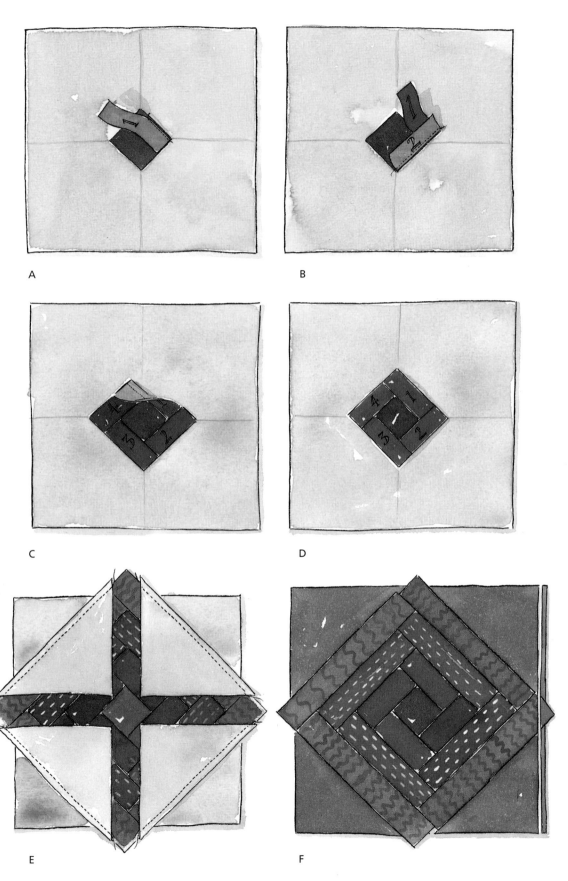

A

B

C

D

E

F

1 Mark the middle lines on the square of wadding both ways with a felt-tip pen. Cut a 4½in (12cm) square of the bright floral fabric and pin it diagonally to the wadding as shown in Fig. A.

2 From the gold fabric cut four strips 2½in (6.5cm) wide and 6½in (17cm) long. Sew the first strip to the middle square (see Fig. A), taking a ¼in (6mm) seam allowance and leaving about the first 1½in (4cm) unsewn. Press the strip outward. Sew on the next strip of gold fabric as shown in Fig. B. Sew on the remaining strips of gold fabric in clockwise order, pressing each strip outward as you are sewing. Pin the unsewn end of the first strip over the fourth strip as shown in Fig. C and sew up to the first line of stitches. Press strip outward with steam iron (see Fig. D).

3 Cut strips from the red fabric to the same width as the gold fabric, but make them about 10½in (27cm) long. Sew them on as Step 2, working out from the gold.

4 Cut strips from the green fabric to the same width, but about 12½in (32cm) long. Sew them on next to the red as Step 2.

5 Cut a 10in (26cm) square from the brown fabric. Fold the square diagonally both ways and cut on the fold lines to make four triangles. Pin the triangles to the block (see Fig. E), sew, and press back outward.

6 Trim the block to 16in (41cm) square (see Fig. F) and zig-zag stitch around the raw edges.

7 Make up the cushion cover with toning fabric, adding a back zip opening as described on p. 21, then insert the cushion pad.

MATERIALS

finished size: 15in (38cm) square

16in (41cm) square of 4oz (100g) polyester wadding

1 fat eighth (*see p. 8*) each of floral print and four gold, red, green and brown cotton print fabrics

16in x 18in (41cm x 46cm) square of toning cotton fabric for back

Felt-tip pen, rotary cutter (*see pp. 10–11*), quilter's ruler, cutting mat, matching sewing cotton, steam iron

12in (30cm) matching zip

15in (38cm) square cushion pad

EASY LEVEL

QUILT-AS-YOU-GO CUSHION

This cushion is very easy to make, but is no less attractive for its simplicity. It can really stand out when placed on a plain-coloured sofa or you can make a feature of it on a bed with a white or cream bedspread. You can also try placing it on an old wooden chair in the kitchen to give it renewed life and some added colour and texture.

The technique is similar to that of Log Cabin (*see Log Cabin Tweed Cushion pp. 50–51*) except that four strips of each colour are sewn around the middle patch as if it is "woven". The middle square can be a scrap of fabric left over from your curtain making, while the four surrounding strips could be self-colour prints in colours picked out from the floral piece.

The fabric strips are pieced directly onto a square of wadding, so you are in fact quilting the cushion top as you sew the patchwork. With piecing by sewing machine, it only takes about 20 minutes to complete the top.

You can use the same method of patchwork to create a large quilt. Just make as many blocks as you need for the quilt and simply stitch them together. Then add some backing fabric and quilt by hand along the seams where all the blocks join.

EASY LEVEL

AMISH CUSHIONS

When you use the R.I.T. Square method of sewing patchwork together (*see pp. 12–13*), it is often just as easy to make two or more blocks as it is to make one. This is the case with these two Amish cushions – a traditional Star block, shown in the photograph, and a Diamond block, shown on page 49. They both have the same middle pattern, but the outer patches have different colours and pattern arrangements.

To follow the Amish tradition, choose plain, bright colours for these cushions, such as fuchsia, magenta, black, royal blue, aqua, scarlet and purple. The Amish people always avoided yellow and white. For a stunning larger project, you could repeat the blocks to create your own quilt design.

MATERIALS
(to make two cushions)
finished size: 15in (38cm)
square

8 fat eighths *(see p. 8)* of royal blue, turquoise, bright pink, black, maroon, scarlet, purple and lilac cotton fabric

½yd (0.45m) of 45in (115cm) wide toning blue cotton fabric for back and piping

Two pieces of 4oz (100g) polyester wadding 16in (41cm) square

No.2 and No.3 templates from the 3-inch set of R.I.T. Squares *(see pp. 108–109)*

Ballpoint or fine felt-tip pen

Rotary cutter *(see pp. 10–11)*

Quilter's ruler, cutting mat

Matching sewing cotton

Steam iron

Quilting materials *(see pp. 16–17)*

3½yd (3.2m) of No.4 piping cord

2 matching 12in (30cm) zips

2 15in (38cm) square cushion pads

1 Make enough No.3 R.I.T. Square patches for both cushions as follows. Place the pieces of royal blue and turquoise fabric right sides together. Using the No.3 R.I.T. Square template as a guide, draw a grid of four squares on the turquoise fabric *(see Fig. A)*. Sew and cut as described on pages 12–13. All seams are ¼in (6mm). Join to make eight No.3 patches.

2 Make the patches for the Star block. From the black and bright pink fabrics, cut pieces 9in x 11in (about 23cm x 28cm) and place right sides together. Using the No.2 R.I.T. Square template, draw a grid of four squares on bright pink fabric *(see Fig. B)*. Sew and cut as described on pages 12–13 to make eight No.2 patches. Cut four 3½in (9cm)

squares from the black fabric to make No.1 patches. Lay the patches for the Star block on the table as in Fig. C, making sure that you have the patches the right way round. Sew them together in rows. Press seams of alternate rows in opposite direction with a steam iron. Sew the rows together matching seams. Press block.

3 From the maroon fabric, cut four strips 2¼in (6cm) wide. Cut two strips to the width of the block and sew to top and bottom. Cut two more strips exactly the length of the block and sew to each side. Press seams outward. Make the No.1 and No.2 patches for the Diamond block exactly as described in Step 2 above, but use the scarlet and purple fabrics. Assemble them as shown in Fig. D. Use the lilac fabric to make the border. Press the block.

4 Now quilt your cushion blocks. Place each piece of patchwork on a square of wadding and pin to secure. Quilt by hand in straight lines about ¼in (6mm) away from the seams in the areas shown in the photographs. The colour of the quilting thread can either match or contrast the patchwork. Mark a centred 16in (41cm) square on the quilted blocks, trim away any excess material, and zig-zag stitch around the edges of the blocks.

5 From the blue backing fabric, cut two pieces 16in x 18in (41cm x 46cm). From the remainder of the blue fabric, cut eight strips 1¼in (3.5cm) wide for the piping. Join and prepare the piping *(see p. 21)*, and sew to the patchwork with raw edges lined up. Make up the cushion covers with back zip openings as described on page 21. Insert the cushion pads.

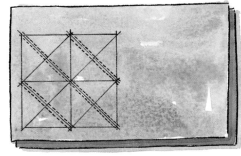

A

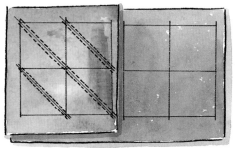

B

C

D

MATERIALS

**finished size: 22in (56cm)
square**

10–12 pieces of wool tweed in
grey, brown and beige, half in
light tones and half in dark

5in (13cm) square of red wool
fabric

4 12in (30cm) squares of
mediumweight cotton fabric
for foundations

24in x 26in (61cm x 66cm)
piece of toning wool fabric for
back

Rotary cutter (*see pp. 10–11*)

Quilter's ruler

Cutting mat

Two bulldog clips

Steam iron

Matching sewing cotton

18in (45cm) matching zip

22in (56cm) cushion pad

A

C

B

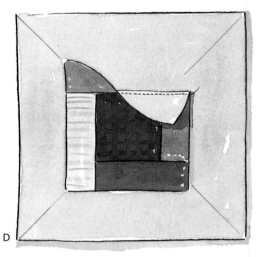

D

1 From the wool fabric pieces
cut 2in (5cm) wide strips for
the logs. You need about 8yd
(7.3m) of dark strips and the same
of light strips. It doesn't matter
how long the strips are because
you are going to cut pieces of
different lengths at random.
Organize the lights and darks by
clipping together with bulldog
clips. Cut four 2½in (6.5cm)
squares from the piece of red wool
fabric. Set up your steam iron near
to your sewing table, so that you
can easily press the seams you're
making as you go along.

2 Take one of the foundation
squares and fold it diagonally
each way. Pin a red square to the
middle (*see Fig. A*).

3 Choose one of the dark strips
for the first log at random.
Chop it off so it is at least as long
as the square (don't measure it
exactly). Pin and sew it right sides
together on top of the red square
(*see Fig. B*) carefully aligning the
raw edges. Take ¼in (6mm) seams
unless otherwise noted. Press the
log outward.

4 Cut next log at random from
the dark strips and chop it so
it is long enough to cover the first
two pieces (*see Fig. C*). Pin and
sew it on as in Step 3. Press the
log outward. Chopping the next
two logs from the light-coloured
strips, continue sewing on logs in
clockwise order (*see Fig. D*). As the
log cabin grows, it is important to

ensure that you are sewing the
logs on straight. Continue
matching the raw edges of the
previous log, but as the block gets
bigger, use your quilter's ruler or
an ordinary ruler to check that the
logs are parallel with those on the
other side.

5 Continue picking two darks
and two lights at random from
your fabric strips until you have
sewn on three rows of strips all the
way around the block (*see Fig. E*).
Make three more log cabin blocks
in the same way. The blocks
should measure about 11½in
(29cm) square. Now sew the four
blocks together, placing them as
shown in the main photograph so
that no two identical dark strips

are adjacent. Sew blocks together
in pairs and then sew the pairs
together, matching up the middle
seam. Clip the seam if necessary,
so it is not too bulky in the middle,
and press well.

6 To make the cushion cover a
little bigger, you can make a
border with four strips of wool
fabric about 1½in (4cm) wide. Cut
two strips to the cover's width and
sew to top and bottom. Cut two
more strips to the cover's length
and sew to each side. If the wool is
on the flimsy side, use some of the
foundation fabric to line the strips
as you sew them on. Press well.
Make up cushion cover with a
back zip opening as described on
page 21. Insert the cushion pad.

E

LOG CABIN TWEED CUSHION

This comfortable Log Cabin cushion proves that you can use heavy wool tweeds just as successfully as pretty florals for an attractive patchwork article. The darker colours used for the cushion will blend particularly well with a faded sofa or a well-worn armchair.

All the wool fabric can be scavenged from jumble sales or fabric shops and pieced together onto a cloth foundation to add stability and keep the "logs" straight. You need enough pieces to cut about 16yd (15m) of 2in (5cm) strips in a range of light tones and dark tones. The "hearth" middle of each block is a square of red wool fabric.

BORDER DESIGN BOLSTER CUSHION

Cushions don't always have to be square, nor do they have to be made in safe pastel colours. Be bold and adventurous with this stunning bolster. Place it among some other square cushions in toning colours to make the most impact.

The wide borders are composed of No.3 R.I.T. Square patches (*see pp. 12–13*) in three different colours. By placing the patches in opposite directions along each row, you can create an interesting pattern of diamonds. The fabrics specified are 45in (115cm) wide unless otherwise noted.

1 First make the border of R.I.T. Squares. Cut two pieces from the magenta fabric and one piece from the floral print about 9in x 13in (23cm x 32cm). Place one magenta piece right sides together with the floral piece. Use the No.3 R.I.T. Square template to draw a grid of six squares on the back of the magenta piece (*see Fig. A*). Sew and cut as described on pages 12–13 to make 24 half-patches. All seams are ¼in (6mm) unless otherwise noted. Press seams with a steam iron toward the darker sides. Repeat with second magenta piece and the texture-print fabric (*see Fig. B*). Separate half-patches into mirror-image piles and sew together as shown in Fig. C to make 24 No.3 patches. Place the

patches as shown in Fig. D to make three borders of eight patches each. Press and block borders.

2 From the purple fabric, cut six strips 1¼in (3.5cm) wide to the same length as the patchwork borders. Sew a strip to each side of the borders, taking care not to stretch them as you sew them on.

3 From the wavy striped fabric, cut two strips 2in (5cm) wide and two strips 1½in (4cm) wide; cut all the same length as the patchwork borders. Sew the wider strips between the rows and the narrower strips to each end. As you sew, make sure that the patchwork's seams are in line across the rows. Press patchwork

MATERIALS

finished size: 18in (46cm) long and 7in (18cm) in diameter

1 fat quarter (*see p. 8*) each of plain magenta and toning floral print cotton fabric

1 fat eighth (*see p. 8*) of dark-magenta texture-print cotton fabric

¼yd (0.25m) each of purple and wavy-striped cotton fabric

No.3 template from the 3-inch set of R.I.T. Squares (*see pp. 108–109*)

Ballpoint or felt-tip pen

Rotary cutter (*see pp. 10–11*)

Quilter's ruler

Cutting mat

Matching sewing cotton

Steam iron

14in (35cm) matching zip

Bolster pad 7in (18cm) in diameter and 18in (46cm) long

well. Stay-stitch along the two shorter sides ¼in (6mm) away from the raw edges.

4 Fold the patchwork in half across width with right sides together and sew with a ⅜in (1cm) seam to make a tube, but leaving an opening of 14in (35cm) for the zip. Press the seam open. Sew zip into the opening. Stay stitch around each end ¼in (6mm) away from the raw edges. Mark the quarter points round the two ends, and clip up to stay-stitching.

5 From floral print fabric, cut two circles 7½in (19cm) in diameter. Mark quarter points around the circle. Turn the bolster cover wrong side out and open zip. Pin one of circles right sides together inside one end of the bolster, matching up quarter points. Sew just inside the stay-stitching, easing if necessary. Repeat with other end; press. Turn right side out and insert pad.

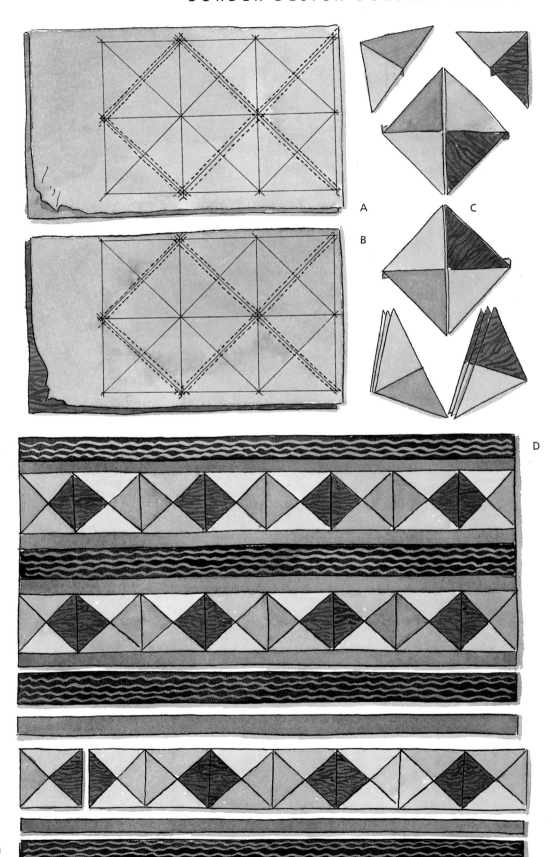

A B C D

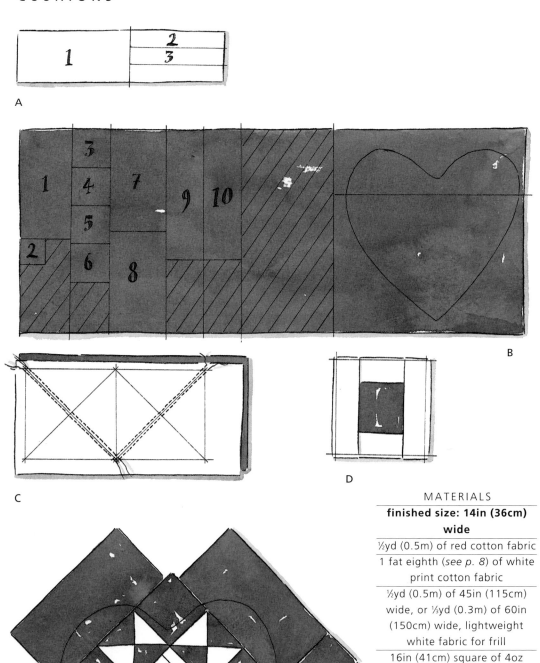

A

B

C

D

E

MATERIALS

finished size: 14in (36cm) wide

½yd (0.5m) of red cotton fabric

1 fat eighth (*see p. 8*) of white print cotton fabric

½yd (0.5m) of 45in (115cm) wide, or ⅓yd (0.3m) of 60in (150cm) wide, lightweight white fabric for frill

16in (41cm) square of 4oz (100g) polyester wadding

Tracing paper, No.1 and No.3 templates from 3-inch set of R.I.T. Squares (*see pp. 108–109*)

Ballpoint pen, rotary cutter (*see pp. 10–11*)

Quilter's ruler, cutting mat, matching sewing cotton, steam iron, water-erasable pen, pins

Red cotton for machine embroidery, clear adhesive tape, 10in (25cm) zip, heart-shaped cushion pad 14in (36cm) wide

1 Draw a template from the heart-shaped pad on this page onto paper and cut out. Draw a line down the middle. Make four No.3 R.I.T. Square patches. From each of red and white print fabrics, cut a piece 5in x 10in (13cm x 25cm) (*see Figs. A1 and B1*). Place two pieces right sides together. Use No.3 R.I.T. Square template to draw a grid of two squares on back of white print (*see Fig. C*). Sew and cut, then join to make No.3 patches (*see pp. 12–13*). All seams are ¼in (6mm) unless otherwise stated.

2 From red print fabric, cut four No.1 R.I.T. Square patches 3½in x 3½in (9cm x 9cm) (*see Figs. B3, 4, 5 and 6*). Make middle patch as follows: cut a 2in (5cm) square from red print fabric (*see Fig. B2*) and two strips 1½in (4cm) wide and about 8in (20cm) long from white print fabric (*see Figs. A2 and 3*). From one of white strips cut two pieces 2in (5cm) long and sew to each side of the 2in (5cm) red square. Press seams outward with a steam iron. Then cut two white strips to same length as resulting piece and sew to other two sides. Press seams outward. Trim patch on sides to match No.1 and No.3 R.I.T. Square patches (*see Fig. D*).

3 Lay out patches in a nine-patch block (*see Fig. E*). Sew together to form three rows. Press seams of Rows 1 and 3 outward, and seams of Row 2 inward. Sew three rows together, matching seams. Press block well. From red print fabric, cut two pieces 5in (13cm) wide and 9in (23cm) long (*see Figs. B7 and 8*). Sew to block (*see Fig. E*). Press seams outward. Cut two more pieces from red print fabric 3½in (9cm) wide and about 12in (30cm) long (*see Figs. B9 and 10*). Sew to block (*see Fig. E*).

Press seams outward. (Adjust strip sizes accordingly for different-sized pad). Lay heart-shaped paper template over patchwork with middle line central and with patchwork design in middle of the heart (*see Fig. E*). Use a water-erasable pen to trace template onto patchwork, then cut out adding a ⅝in (1.5cm) seam allowance. Cut some wadding to the same size.

4 Pin patchwork block to wadding for quilting. Thread machine with red cotton and stitch around the patchwork "star" about ⅟₂₅in (1mm) away from seams. If preferred, decorate white middle section with fancy machine embroidery, using a water-erasable pen to draw guidelines.

5 Make frill from white fabric. Cut strips 6in (15cm) wide to make 120in (3m). Join strips to make a circle. Fold in half lengthways and press. To decorate frill edge with fancy machine embroidery, open up folded strip and stitch all around with the edge of the presser foot against the fold line. Fold circular strip in half again lengthways and mark halfway points with two pins. Gather frill to fit heart's circumference. Pin to cushion top so that gathering line matches line marked around the heart, with pins at top and bottom. Sew frill to cushion top just inside gathering line.

6 Make up cushion back. From red print fabric, cut a rectangle 1in (2.5cm) wider and 2in (5cm) longer than template (*see Fig. B*). Insert zip (*see p. 21*). Use heart template to cut out back, adding ⅝in (1.5cm) seam allowance. Pin cushion back and front right sides together, holding frill away from seam with clear adhesive tape. Sew on stitching line with wadding side upward. Open zip, turn cushion cover right sides out and insert pad.

VALENTINE CUSHION

Heart-shaped cushions have a special charm and this unashamedly romantic one is no exception. Make it for your loved one as a surprise present on St Valentine's Day or perhaps for your wedding anniversary.

Use the R.I.T. Square method (*see pp. 12–13*) to create the star block in the middle. A red print cotton fabric is the obvious choice for the main part of the heart shape, with white fabric to set it off. Sew a wide frill around the edge of the cushion to give a beautiful finish. If your sewing machine does fancy machine embroidery, you can add a border around the middle and on the frill for an extra flourish if you wish. All the fabrics specified for the cushion are 45in (115cm) wide unless otherwise noted.

A

B

C

D

E

F

G

H

I

1 Make chevron band as follows. (Ideally use imperial measurements throughout this project.) Cut four strips each from the yellow and turquoise fabrics ¾in (2cm) wide and four from the crimson fabric 1in (2.5cm) wide. Sew the strips together to make four strip sets of the three colours as shown in Fig. A. All the seams are ¼in (6mm) unless otherwise noted. Press all seams with a steam iron in one direction and then block strip the sets so that they are perfectly straight.

2 Use your quilter's ruler and rotary cutter to cut the strip sets at a 45° angle and 1¾in (4.5cm) wide (see Fig. A). Line up the 45° angle line of the ruler to one of the grid lines of your cutting mat for accuracy. Cut two of the strip sets angled toward the right and two angled toward the left. You can cut six pieces from each strip set. Sew the pieces together (see Fig. B) to make two long bands. Press and block all seams of one band to the right, and those of the other to the left (see Fig. C).

3 Trim each band to measure 1½in (4cm). Cut off angled section from the right-hand end and sew to the left-hand end to make ends straight. Sew the two bands together, using pins if necessary to make sure the stripes match up. Press middle seam open and block the band. Cut band to 12½in (32cm). From the royal blue fabric, cut two strips 12½in (32cm) long and ¾in (2cm) wide. Sew them both to each side of the chevron band.

4 Make zig-zag band as follows. Cut four strips of yellow fabric 1¼in (3.2cm) wide; four strips of royal blue fabric 1in (2.5cm) wide; and two strips of fuchsia fabric ¾in

(2cm) wide. Sew the three colours together to make two strip sets as shown in Fig. D. Place strips of one set to the right and the other to the left. Press seams of one strip upward and the seams of the other strip downward. Block the strip sets so that they are straight.

5 Cut pieces from strip sets at a 60° angle and 1½in (4cm) wide. Line up 60° angle line of the ruler with one of the grid lines of your cutting mat for accuracy. Cut one of the strip sets angled toward the right and the other angled toward the left. (You can cut the pieces from both strip sets at the same time by placing one upside down on top of the other.) You get about nine pieces from each strip set.

6 Sew pieces together alternately to make the zig-zag band (see Fig. E). To line up seams, put a pin through ¼in (6mm) away from the raw edges of the pieces exactly where the seams should meet. Trim band exactly ½in (1.3cm) away from the tips of the blue points (see Fig. F). Press and block band, and then cut to 12½in (32cm). From turquoise fabric, cut two strips 12½in (32cm) long and ¾in (2cm) wide. Sew to each side of the zig-zag band.

7 Make the woven band from two different strip sets as follows. For the first-strip set, cut two strips of turquoise fabric ¾in (2cm) wide, one strip of turquoise fabric 1¼in (3.2cm) wide and two strips of yellow fabric 1in (2.5cm) wide. For the second strip set, cut two strips of royal blue fabric 1½in (4cm) wide and one strip of fuchsia fabric ¾in (2cm) wide. Sew together to make two strip sets as shown in figs. G and H. Press all seams outward from the narrower

MATERIALS

finished size: 12in (30cm) square

1 fat quarter (*see p. 8*) each of yellow, turquoise, crimson, royal blue, fuchsia and black cotton fabrics
Rotary cutter (*see pp. 10–11*)
Quilter's ruler
Cutting mat
Matching sewing cotton
Steam iron, pins
1½yd (1.25m) No.4 piping cord
10in (25cm) black zip
12in (30cm) square cushion pad

strips and block strip sets so they are straight.

8 Cut each strip set into pieces 1in (2.5cm) wide as shown in figs. G and H. Sew pieces together alternately, taking care that the fuchsia stripe is in line across the band (*see Fig. I*). Press and block the band well, then cut to 12½in (32cm) long.

9 From crimson fabric cut two strips 12½in (32cm) long and ¾in (2cm) wide. Sew to each side of woven band. From black fabric cut two strips 12½in (32cm) long and 1¼in (3.2cm) wide. Sew between the three bands as shown in the photograph. Cut two black strips 12½in (32cm) long and 2in (5cm) wide and sew to top and bottom of the block. Press well. Trim finished cushion block to 12½in (32cm) square.

10 Cut cushion back and piping strips from the remaining black fabric, then prepare the piping (*see p. 21*) and sew to the patchwork top with raw edges lined up. Make up the back with a zip opening (*see p. 21*), trim back to 12½in (34cm) square and sew back to cushion top. Insert cushion pad.

SEMINOLE CUSHION

Three different Seminole bands are sewn together to make this bright cushion. Seminole patchwork involves joining long strips of fabric and cutting them into smaller pieces which are then sewn together in various ways to create hundreds of different "band" designs. This technique was developed by the Seminole Indians, a group of native Americans who were forcibly resettled to swampy areas of Florida in the late nineteenth century. On acquiring hand- or treadle-operated sewing machines around this time, the Seminole women began to create designs or patchwork with brightly dyed cotton fabrics, based on geometric beadwork designs. These were then sewn into garments such as skirts and tops for women and shirts for men. Many items were sold as tourist curios. Contemporary quick-piecing techniques have their roots in Seminole patchwork, but unfortunately Seminole craftswomen had no rotary-cutting equipment to make their job easier!

Save your leftover bits from this project and use them to make pincushions, Christmas cards, Christmas tree ornaments and a Christmas stocking in Home Accessories (*see pp. 78–107*). You can also decorate guest towels, curtains and clothing with Seminole bands. Note that the strips for the pieced bands in the cushion are cut across the width of fat quarters of fabric, so they are all 18in (45cm) long.

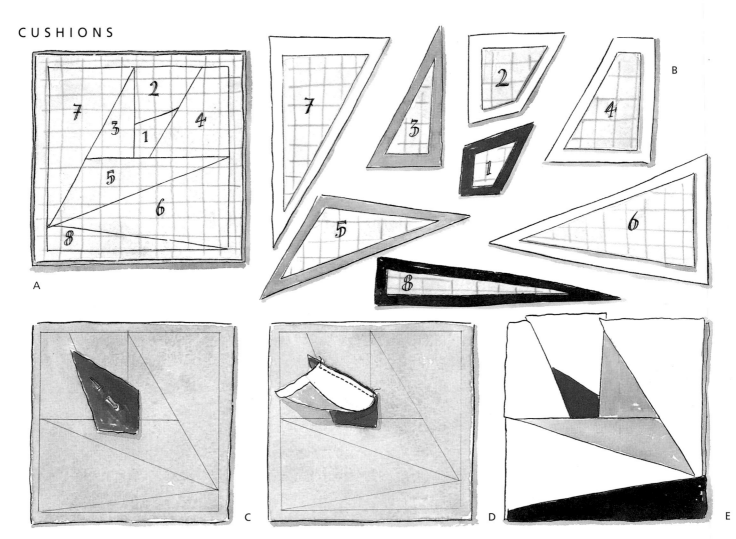

A

B

C

D

E

MATERIALS

(to make two cushions)

finished size: 15in (38cm) square

1 fat quarter (*see p. 8*) each of light- and deep-yellow and white cotton fabric

Big scrap of dark-blue cotton

½yd (0.5m) of royal blue cotton fabric for borders and backs

⅜yd (0.6m) white firmly woven cotton fabric for foundations (*see pp. 14–15*)

2 16in (40cm) squares of 2oz (50g) polyester wadding

Photocopied design, spray starch

Light box, fine-tipped pen, ruler

Scissors, clear adhesive tape, matching sewing cotton

Table lamp, pins, steam iron, 2 12in (30.5cm) matching zips

3½yd (3.2m) No.4 piping cord

2 15in (38cm) cushion pads

1 Cut eight 7in (18cm) squares of foundation cloth. Enlarge Fig. F to twice its size (200%) on a photocopier to make master design. Transfer onto backs of the cloth foundations with a light box (*see Fig. A*), or put on a window. (Tracing is easier if foundations are spray starched.) Number areas as shown.

2 Cut numbered areas of paper master design along lines to make templates. Stick these to reverse side of appropriate coloured fabrics using rolled-up tape. For each block cut out eight fabric pieces around paper templates, leaving a seams margin of at least ⅜in (8mm) (*see Fig. B*).

3 Remove paper template from Piece 1. Use your table lamp to check that you have correctly

placed the piece right side up on the blank side of the foundation squares so that it covers Area 1. Pin in place (*see Fig. C*).

4 Take Piece 2 and, using your lamp to check its position, place it right side down over Piece 1 so that the edge of the paper template is on the line between Areas 1 and 2. Remove the template and then pin Piece 2 in position. From the back of the foundation square (i.e. on the side with the printed lines), sew on that line (*see Fig. D*). Remove pin and fold Piece 2 over to cover Area 2. Check with the light that it is correctly positioned. Then fold Piece 2 back over Piece 1 again and trim the seam almost to the sewing line. Fold Piece 2 back over Area 2 and press well.

5 Repeat Step 4 with all eight pieces until first block is complete (*see Fig. E*). Sew around block just outside square. Make four blocks in this way for each cushion. Join blocks, matching up seams. Cut strips 2in (5cm) wide and 18in (45cm) long from royal blue fabric. Cut two strips to block's width and sew to top and bottom. Cut two more strips to block's length and sew to sides.

6 Pin patchwork to a square of wadding. Quilt around edges of white blocks using the "stitch-in-the-ditch" technique (*see p. 17*). Using deep-yellow fabric, prepare piping and sew to cushion fronts (*see p. 21*). Make up the cushion covers with back material, inserting a back zip opening (*see p. 21*). Insert cushion pads.

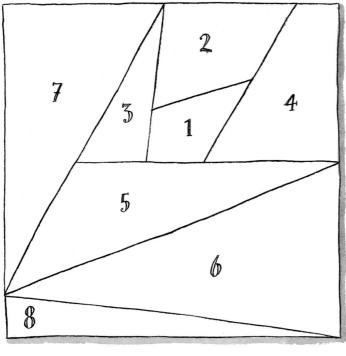

F

ADVANCED LEVEL

WATER LILY FOUNDATION CUSHIONS

These delightful cushions will give a summery atmosphere to any living room or bedroom. Four water lily blocks make up the cushions, pieced using the foundation method (*see pp. 14–15*). A cloth foundation is used here rather than paper, because it adds the extra stability needed for this larger design.

For a smaller project, you could scale the design down by half to make a delightful quilt for a doll's bed. For convenience, set up your work table with a lamp and have a steam iron nearby before you begin the project. All the fabric specified is 45in (115cm) wide unless otherwise stated.

PERSONAL ACCESSORIES

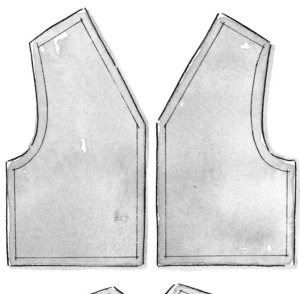

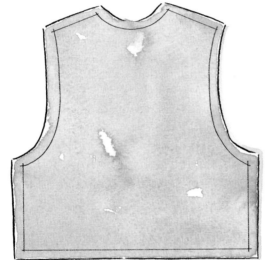

A

MATERIALS

Assortment of silk pieces to make 32 strips 2in x 22in (5cm x 60cm)
⅝yd (0.6m) of 60in (150cm) wide toning lining fabric
⅝yd (0.6m) of 45in (115cm) wide soft cotton fabric for interlining
Waistcoat pattern
Scissors
Rotary cutter (*see pp. 10–11*)
Quilter's ruler
Cutting mat
Matching sewing thread
Steam iron
Silver metallic thread for machine quilting
Waistcoat buckle and buttons (as required)

1 Using the waistcoat pattern, cut a back and a left and right front from the cotton interlining, including the normal ⅝in (1.5cm) seam allowances (*see Fig. A*).

2 From your assortment of silk pieces, cut strips 2in (5cm) wide. If a silk strip is too short, you can join two different lengths together to add interest to the waistcoat, seaming them as Fig. B.

3 Taking ¼in (6mm) seams, sew the strips together to form "strippy" sheets large enough to cover the three interlining pieces plus about 1in (2.5cm) over all the way around (*see Fig. C*). You need about eight strips to cover each front piece, and about 15 strips for the back. Choose the strips more or less at random, but with some contrast of pattern and colour. Occasionally introduce a diagonally pieced strip. Press the seams open with a steam iron.

4 Thread your sewing machine with silver metallic thread. Pin the strippy sheets to the interlining pieces and quilt through the interlining with straight lines of stitching just to the left of the seam lines. Trim away the excess patchwork level with the edges of the interlining (*see Fig. D*).

5 Make up waistcoat according to pattern. You can use leftover pieces to make a matching Strippy Silk Clutch Bag (*see pp. 66–67*).

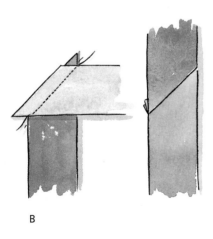

B

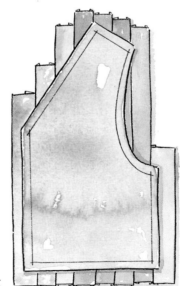

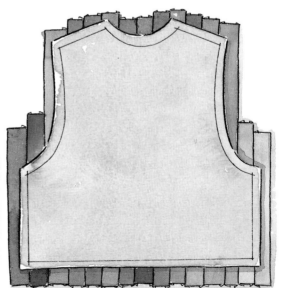

C

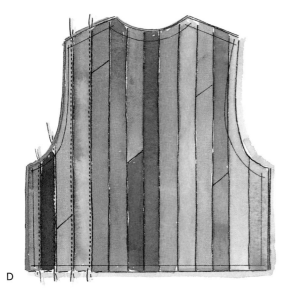

EASY LEVEL

STRIPPY SILK WAISTCOAT

This waistcoat is made from beautiful silk pieces from Japan. You could use any pretty silk scraps, silk sample pieces or even cast-off ties. The waistcoat would also be striking in some of the new ethnic or metallic prints available in patchwork shops.

Use a paper pattern to make up your waistcoat. The waistcoat pictured above is size 14 and contains a variety of silks about 6in x 22in (16cm x 60cm). If your pattern is larger, you will need to use more fabric.

STRIPPY SILK CLUTCH BAG

Sew a matching clutch bag from silk pieces left over from the Strippy Waistcoat on pages 64-65. Decorated with metallic thread and a novel "croissant" toggle button, it makes a really elegant accessory for an evening out.

The silk bag is so easy to piece together that you could run up several at the same time and give them to friends as presents. If the bag was made in more practical, washable fabrics, it would also be perfect to use as a cosmetic bag.

1 Cut eight silk strips 2in (5cm) wide and about 16in (40cm) long. Lay the first strip on the interlining, overlapping the left-hand edge by about ½in (1.3cm). Choose the next strip at random, but with some contrast of colour and pattern. Lay it right sides together over the first strip and sew through interlining ¼in (6mm) away from the right-hand edge of the strips. Press the second strip over to the right with a steam iron.

2 Continue sewing on the rest of the strips in this way (see Fig. A) until the entire piece of interlining is covered. Press well. Now decorate the patchwork piece

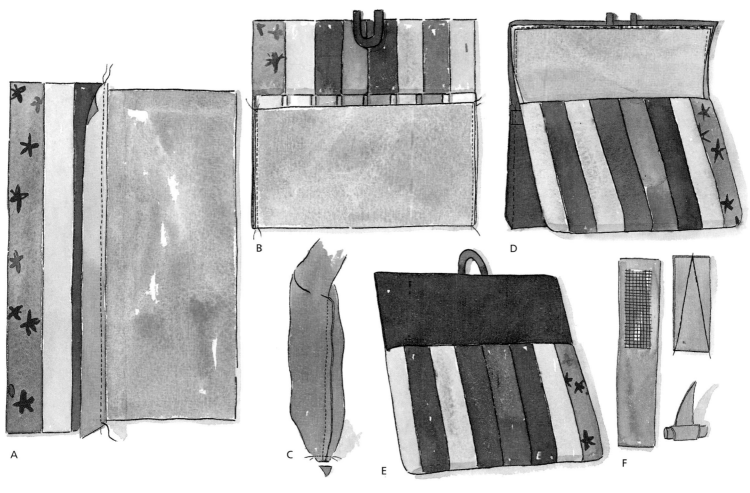

A

B

C

D

E

F

MATERIALS

finished size: 10in x 5in (24cm x 12.5cm)

2in x 32in (5cm x 80cm) silk strips in each of four patterns
10in x 15in (25cm x 38cm) craft-weight non-woven interlining or pelmet interlining
10½in x 15½in (27cm x 40cm) brightly coloured silk for lining
Scrap of silk for fastening loop
1½in x 8in (4cm x 20cm) silk strip for toggle
1½in x 4in (4cm x 10cm) fusible web
Rotary cutter (see pp. 10–11)
Quilter's ruler
Cutting mat
Matching sewing thread
Steam iron
Metallic thread for quilting
Clear adhesive tapes

with some metallic thread sewn in a zig-zag stitch over the seam lines of all the silk strips.

3 Fold the patchwork right sides together to make a pocket 5½in (14 cm) deep and stitch very close to the interlining (see Fig. B). Turn the raw patchwork edge over the interlining. "Sew off" a little triangle from the wrong side at each corner (see Fig. C), trim off the corner, and turn right side out.

4 Cut the lining to the same size as the patchwork. Turn under the top edge of the lining pocket by ½in (1.3cm) and press. Sew each side of the lining pocket as in

Step 3, but increase seam slightly so that the lining will be a little smaller than the bag. "Sew off" corners as previously.

5 To make a fastening loop, cut a scrap of silk that measures 2½in x ¾in (6.5cm x 2cm). Fold it in half lengthwise and then carefully fold the raw edges into the middle. Sew the folded edges together by hand with neat stitches. Hold the loop in place on the bag with a piece of clear tape.

6 With right sides together, sew the flap of the patchwork to the flap of the lining, around three sides, very close to the interlining,

catching the fastening loop in the seam (see Fig. D). Trim the corners, turn right side out and push the lining into patchwork pocket (see Fig. E). Sew the folded edge of the lining to the inside of the pocket.

7 Apply the fusible web to half the length of the silk strip for the toggle as shown in Fig. F. Remove the paper backing and then fold the other half of the silk strip over and iron to create a double thickness. Cut a long triangle as shown. Roll up from the wide end as if you were making a croissant. Fix the point in position with a tiny scrap of fusible web. Finally, sew toggle onto bag.

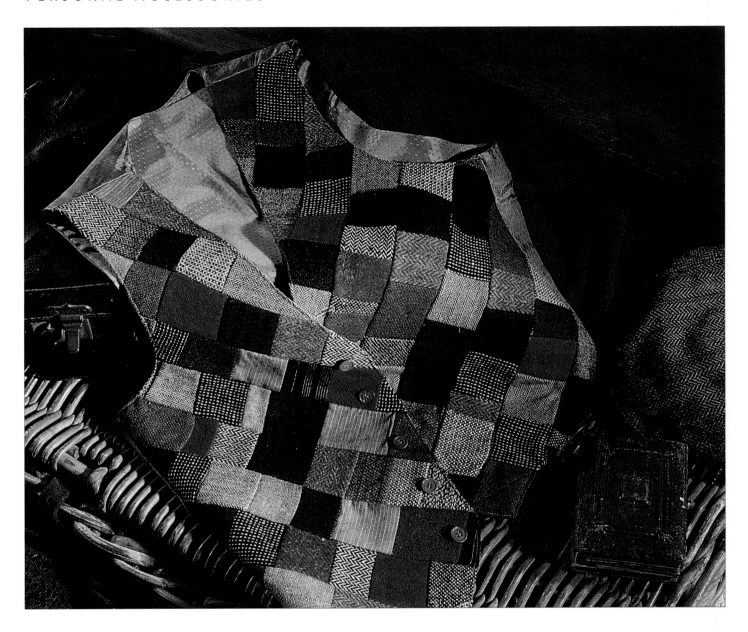

MAN'S WOOL WAISTCOAT

Waistcoats are a popular fashion accessory. Children want them in bright novelty prints, teenagers want them for school or college, women want them for evening wear and, finally, men want them. The favourite man in your life would gladly exchange his pin-striped version for this rustic weekend waistcoat, made from wool fabrics gleaned from jumble sales. Only the fronts are made from patchwork; the back is made from some lining fabric.

Wool can be difficult to use for patchwork, because its heavy weight makes very bulky seams. It does require a lot of pressing with a steam iron, but the bulk of the seams adds an interesting texture to the patchwork, which does not then need to be quilted. Make sure that you press all the seams well in the same direction.

Use a paper pattern in the required size to make up the waistcoat, remembering to allow enough wool scraps to fit the width of the waistcoat fronts.

1 With pattern, cut a left and right front from interfacing without seam allowances. Draw diagonal lines with pen on the adhesive side of pieces (see Fig. A), to help place patchwork strips.

2 Cut some wool strips 2½in (6cm) wide in a variety of colours. Cut pieces from the wool strips in different lengths from 1½in to 3½in (3cm to 9cm). Pick up small wool pieces at random for a good mix of colour, texture and size and sew together in rows

MATERIALS

¾yd (0.7m) of 35in (90cm) wide mediumweight iron-on interfacing
Wool scraps sufficient to cover two waistcoat fronts
1½yd (1.4m) of 60in (150cm) toning lining fabric
Waistcoat pattern
Scissors
Felt-tip marking pen
Rotary cutter (see pp. 10–11)
Quilter's ruler
Cutting mat
Matching sewing cotton
Steam iron
Waistcoat buckle and buttons (as required)

with ¼in (6mm) seams to cover the waistcoat fronts diagonally.

3 When you have four rows of patchwork pieces, check the lengths against the waistcoat front (see Fig. B). Sew them together so that brighter colours are scattered around, rearranging rows where necessary for a good balance. Press all the seams with a steam iron to one side.

4 Continue making rows of patches, sewing them together until you have enough patchwork for one waistcoat front (see Fig. C). Leave a good margin all around the shape for the seam allowance. Press patchwork well with the steam iron. Repeat for second waistcoat front, slanting strips the other way.

5 Apply the interfacing pieces to the wrong sides of the patchwork. Trim any excess material, making sure you leave a ⅝in (1.5cm) seam allowance (see Fig. D).

6 Make up waistcoat back with lining fabric, and finish following the pattern instructions.

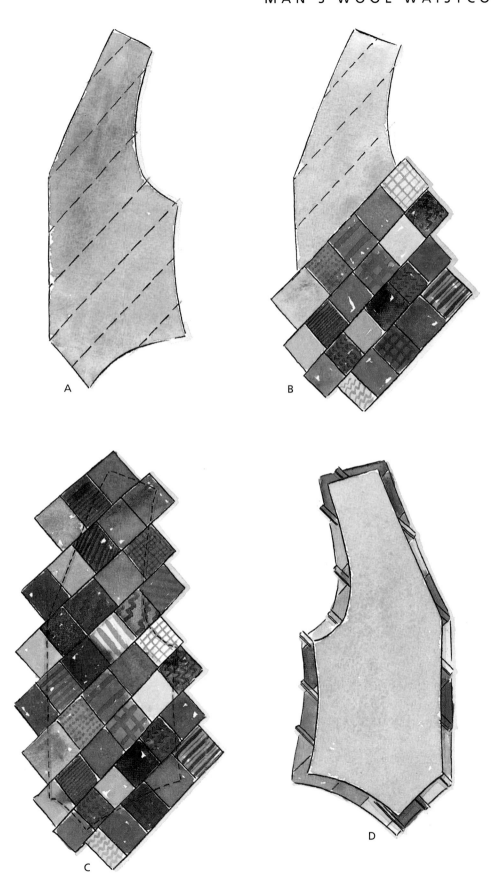

A

B

C

D

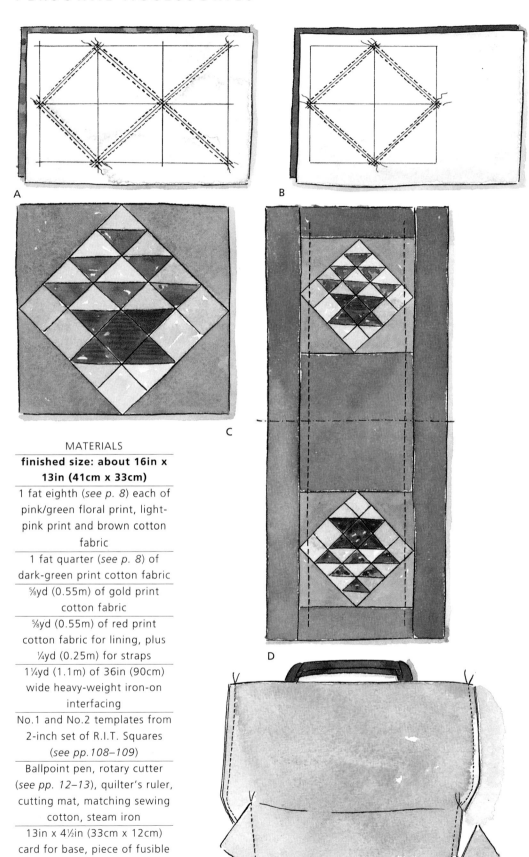

A

B

C

D

E

MATERIALS

finished size: about 16in x 13in (41cm x 33cm)

1 fat eighth (see p. 8) each of pink/green floral print, light-pink print and brown cotton fabric

1 fat quarter (see p. 8) of dark-green print cotton fabric

⅝yd (0.55m) of gold print cotton fabric

⅝yd (0.55m) of red print cotton fabric for lining, plus ¼yd (0.25m) for straps

1¼yd (1.1m) of 36in (90cm) wide heavy-weight iron-on interfacing

No.1 and No.2 templates from 2-inch set of R.I.T. Squares (see pp.108–109)

Ballpoint pen, rotary cutter (see pp. 12–13), quilter's ruler, cutting mat, matching sewing cotton, steam iron

13in x 4½in (33cm x 12cm) card for base, piece of fusible web a bit larger than base

1 Make two basket blocks by placing the pink/green floral print and light-pink print fabrics right sides together. Use the No.2 R.I.T. Square template to draw a grid of six squares on the back of one of them (see Fig. A). Place brown and light-pink print fabrics with right sides together and draw a grid of four squares on the back of one of them (see Fig. B). Sew and cut No.2 patches (see pp. 12–13). All seams are ¼in (6mm) unless otherwise noted. Press seams with a steam iron toward darker side. Now use No.1 template to cut out ten 2½in (6.5cm) squares from the light-pink print fabric and two from the brown.

2 Assemble two 16-patch basket blocks (see Fig. C). Then cut two 9in (23cm) squares from dark-green print fabric. Fold each square diagonally each way and cut on fold lines to make four triangles from each square. Sew four triangles to sides of each basket block (see Fig. C). Press. Trim block to 11½in (29.5cm) square.

3 From gold print fabric, cut a strip 11½in (29.5cm) wide and across fabric width. From this strip cut a piece 12½in x 11½in (32cm x 29.5) and two pieces 4in x 11½in (10cm x 29.5cm). Sew larger piece between the two blocks and the two smaller ones to top and bottom (see Fig. D). From gold print fabric, cut two strips 4in (10cm) wide and about 44in (115cm) long. Trim two strips to patchwork panel length and sew to each side (see Fig. D). Press seams outward.

4 Cut out a piece of interfacing ½in (1cm) smaller than the patchwork panel and then iron centrally to back. Fold panel in half and press a fold line (see Fig. D). Cut out red print fabric for bag's lining to the panel's width but make it 2in (5cm) shorter in length.

5 Cut three 3in (7cm) wide strips from the red print fabric for the straps and then join end to end to make one long strip. Cut 1in (2.5cm) wide strips of iron-on interfacing to fix to the wrong side of the long strap ½in (1cm) away from one of the raw edges. Fold in raw edges on both sides by ½in (1cm) and fold strip in half lengthways. Press. Cut strap to 3¼yd (2.94m) long and sew ends together to make a ring. Stitch near edge on both sides around the ring. Mark halfway points of ring.

6 Sew ring to the panel covering the edges of the patchwork block (depicted by dotted lines in Fig. D) and matching halfway points with the fold line in the panel's middle. Leave straps unsewn at ends of panel by 1½in (4cm). There will be two loops at each end to make the handles.

7 Fold panel right sides together to form a bag and sew up side seams, close to interfacing, but don't sew straps into seam.

8 To square off bag's base, "sew off" corners with stitching 4½in (11cm) long (see Fig. E). Cut off corners. Turn bag right side out.

9 Make lining from red print fabric as in steps 7 and 8. Put lining inside bag wrong sides together and matching side seams. Press inward the top ½in (1cm) of the bag. Turn folded edge in over lining and stitch around edge, but not over straps.

10 Measure the squared-off base and cut some card to fit. Cut a piece of the dark-green print fabric about 1in (2.5cm) larger all around than the card and fix to card with fusible web. Place in bottom of the bag, folding raw edges of fabric over card.

INTERMEDIATE LEVEL

FLOWER BASKET SHOPPING BAG

This handy bag, made in brightly coloured cotton fabrics, is interlined and the straps are sewn right under the base, so it can hold a lot of shopping. It is also suitable for children to carry books to school, and it is of course ideal to transport your sewing kit to a patchwork class.

The bag is decorated with two "Flower Basket" blocks. Flower Basket is a traditional American block pattern and is usually set diagonally with a triangle sewn to each corner so that the flowers don't tip out!

The block pattern is a 16-patch design, and it is made here with the 2-inch set of R.I.T. Squares (see pp. 12–13). The fabrics specified are 45in (115cm) wide unless otherwise noted.

CRAZY PATCH-WORK BACKPACK

This richly coloured backpack will be the envy of all your friends. It is made using the crazy patchwork method (*see p. 14*). Once you get the knack of cutting the irregular pieces, you will find it very quick to sew them onto the foundation. There is something particularly satisfying about selecting the wildest combination of floral, damask and woven geometric patterns to create an absolutely unique bag which is also very practical. After sewing on the crazy patches, you can decorate them with fancy machine embroidery, zig-zag stitching or some attractive hand embroidery.

The beautiful fabrics for this project were obtained from a furnishing shop, where some old sample books and remnants were on sale at a bargain price. As furnishing fabrics are often heavy, it would be a good idea to use a No.14 needle in your sewing machine rather than a No.11, which is the size suitable for most types of patchwork.

If you prefer to make a different style of bag from the one illustrated, there are lots of variations available in different pattern books that are just as suitable for this crazy patchwork method.

1 From furnishing fabric, cut and mark pattern pieces for lining, flap, pocket and base (*see Fig. A1, 2, 3 and 4*).

2 From furnishing fabric samples, cut some crazy patchwork pieces. Choose fabrics with an interesting variety of colour and texture. The pieces should be about 2in (5cm) wide in each direction. Sew crazy patches to adhesive side of the foundation of heavy-weight iron-on interfacing with ¼in (6mm) seams (*see p. 14*), until rectangle is covered, including seam

MATERIALS

finished size: 14in (36cm)
high x 10in (25cm) wide

Selection of furnishing fabric samples

Piece of heavy-weight iron-on interfacing 14in x 30in (36cm x 76cm)

Piece of furnishing fabric for lining 15¼in x 30in (39cm x 75cm)

Two pieces of furnishing fabric 7½in x 7½in (19cm x 19cm) for flap

Piece of furnishing fabric 6½in x 6½in (16.5cm x 16.5cm) for inside pocket

Three pieces of furnishing fabric 5½in x 11in (14cm x 28cm) for base

Scrap of furnishing fabric 3in (7.5cm) long for loop

Rotary cutter (see pp. 10–11), quilter's ruler, cutting mat, matching sewing cotton, steam iron

1yd (0.9m) of ¼in (6mm) diameter twisted cord, large wooden bead with big hole, 6in (15cm) of curtain weights

28in (71cm) of 1in (2.5cm) wide webbing for straps

10in x 4½in (25.5cm x 11.5cm) card for base

Piece of fusible web slightly larger than the card

allowances (see Fig. B). Press crazy patches with a steam iron so that they adhere to the foundation. Use a pressing cloth, if necessary, to protect any fabric that would be damaged by a hot iron. If you wish, decorate the folded edges of the crazy pieces with some machine embroidery.

3 Trim edges of crazy patchwork rectangle even with foundation. Fold patchwork in half, right sides together, and sew a ⅝in (1.5cm) side seam. Press seam open. Stay stitch ⅝in (1.5cm)

away from raw edge around base. Mark centre and quarter points (see Fig. B). Clip up to stay stitching.

4 Turn patchwork inside out and pin one of the base pieces to the bottom edge, right sides together, matching halfway marks. Sew on line of stay stitching, easing around corners.

5 Make a lining with a base, following Steps 3 and 4. Turn over top 1in (2.5cm) of pocket and hem. Turn in raw edges of three sides of pocket and sew to lining (see Fig. A). Turn over top edge of lining by ¼in (6mm) and press. Push lining into the bag, matching up the side seams. Make a little loop 3in (8cm) long from a furnishing scrap. Fold top 1in (2.5cm) of lining over the bag and topstitch close to the fold, stitching in the loop at the front as shown in Fig. C. Mark and sew eight buttonholes 1in (2.5cm) long (see Fig. C). Thread the cord through the buttonholes and loop. Feed two ends of the cord through the wooden bead and knot ends together (see Fig. D).

6 With right sides together, sew flap facing to the flap around three sides. Trim and clip seam, turn right side out and press. Sew curtain weights to inside of flap. Turn in ½in (1cm) along the raw edge of flap toward the facing. Sew flap to bag close to fold, catching in the ends of the straps (see Fig. E). Sew a second line of stitching ¾in (2cm) away as shown, to form a channel to hold the backpack's draw-cord.

7 Trim card so that it fits snugly in the bottom of the bag. Fix the remaining base piece to the card with the fusible web, turning raw edges to back of card edges. To finish, place card in bottom of bag.

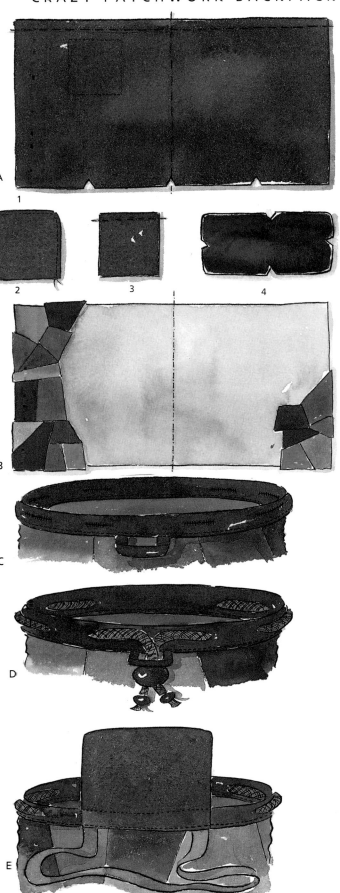

A
1
2
3
4
B
C
D
E

1 Using your waistcoat pattern, cut a left and right front from iron-on interfacing. From the lining fabric cut a left and right front and two backs. Be sure to include seam allowances (*see Fig. A*).

2 From your assorted silky scraps, cut a selection of crazy patchwork pieces. The pieces need to be a minimum of 2in (5cm) wide in each direction.

3 Sew the crazy patches to the adhesive side of the two interfacing pieces with ¼in (6mm) seams (*see p. 14*). Place the patches in such a way that there is an interesting balance of colours and prints on both sides (*see Fig. B*). Once both interfacing fronts are completely covered with crazy patches, including the seam allowances, press the fronts with a steam iron so that the patches bond with the the interfacing. You can then decorate the crazy patches with top-stitching, or with some hand or machine embroidery (*see Fig. C*).

4 Make up the waistcoat's back with lining fabric. Line and finish the waistcoat following the instructions of your pattern.

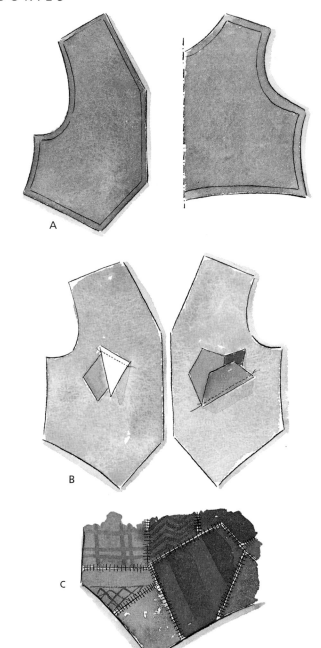

A

B

C

D

MATERIALS
¾yd (0.7m) of 35in (90cm) wide medium-weight iron-on interfacing
1½yd (1.4m) of 45in (115cm) lining fabric
Selection of old silk ties and other silky scraps
Pattern for a lined waistcoat
Rotary cutter (*see pp. 10–11*)
Quilter's ruler
Cutting mat
Matching sewing thread
Steam iron
Waistcoat buckle and buttons (as required)

ADVANCED LEVEL

CRAZY PATCHWORK WAISTCOAT

A silk waistcoat instantly adds style to an outfit. If you stitch one in crazy patchwork, you can use all kinds of interesting silky scraps to create a unique and stunning garment. And if your sewing machine is capable of fancy embroidery stitches, then this project will make good use of every one.

The waistcoat illustrated has a crazy patchwork front and a plain back made from lining fabric. Old silk ties are a rich source of suitable patches; alternatively, silk remnants or even lightweight furnishing fabrics will provide you with a wonderful selection of colours and patterns. Check how many silk scraps you will need against the size of paper pattern you are using to make up the waistcoat.

DOROTHY BAG

Named after the bag carried by Dorothy down the Yellow Brick Road in *The Wizard of Oz*, this style of drawstring bag is both attractive and useful. The glamorous version illustrated is ideal for evening use and is made from crazy patchwork using scraps of decorative, shiny fabrics such as old silk ties, brocades, taffetas and satins. If you want to make a more practical, everyday bag, choose from a selection of pretty, washable, printed cotton fabrics instead.

1 From interfacing and lining fabrics, cut two 12in (30cm) squares. From the interfacing cut one 7in (18cm) diameter circle, and from the lining cut two matching circles.

2 From fabric scraps, cut a few crazy patches, about 2in (5cm) wide in each direction. Sew onto adhesive side of interfacing squares with ¼in (6mm) seams (*see p. 14*). Continue, adding contrasting patches (*see Fig. A*), until interfacing squares and seam allowances are covered. Press with warm iron to bond the patches with the interfacing. Decorate all the edges of the crazy patches with some embroidery stitches. Trim patchwork to same size as interfacing.

3 Mark large and small dots on wrong side of the two crazy patchwork pieces. With right sides together, join side seams up to large dots, taking a ⅝in (1.5cm) seam (*see Fig. B*). Reinforce stitching at large dots and clip seams. Press seams open. Stay-stitch ⅝in (1.5cm) around lower edge and clip up to stitches (*see Fig. B*). Mark halfway points between side seams. Repeat with two lining pieces.

A

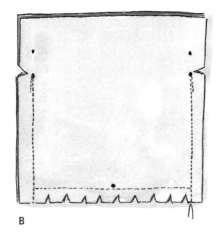

B

C

D

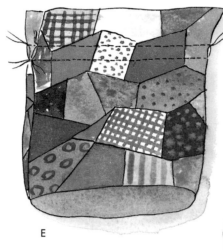

E

F

4 Iron the interfacing circle to the wrong side of one lining circle. Mark the quarter points of the circle (*see Fig. C*). With crazy patchwork bag wrong sides out, place on base with the right sides together, matching quarter marks with the side seams and the halfway marks. Stitch the bag to the base just inside the stay-stitching and press well. Sew bag lining to base in same way, but with a 3in (8cm) opening (*see Fig. D*).

5 With the bag and the lining inside out, place the flaps of the bag right sides together with lining flaps. Face the flaps by sewing around the three sides of the top as far as the small dots, taking a ⅝in (1.5cm) seam (*see Fig. D*). Trim the seams and clip corners. Pull crazy patchwork bag through the opening in lining base and press flaps. Sew up lining opening. With a water-erasable pen, mark stitching lines for channels for the pull-ties on each side of the gaps in the side seams (*see Fig. E*). Stitch carefully along the marked lines.

(60cm) long. Fold the strips in half lengthwise, then open out and press raw edges up to the pressed line. Fold the strip in half again with the raw edges enclosed, fold in the ends and machine down both sides. With the bodkin, feed ends of one tie through both channels of the bag (*see Fig. F*). Feed the ends of the other tie through both channels from other side. Tie together.

6 To make the drawstrings, cut two pieces from the lining or silky fabric 2in (5cm) wide and 24in

MATERIALS
finished size: about 11in (28cm) high
Selection of fabric scraps
½yd (0.3m) of 35in (90cm) wide mediumweight iron-on interfacing
½yd (0.5m) of 60in (152cm) wide matching polyester lining fabric
Rotary cutter (*see pp. 10–11*)
Quilter's ruler
Cutting mat
Matching sewing thread
Iron
Water-erasable pen
Bodkin

HOME ACCESSORIES

MATERIALS

(to make a tray cloth and napkin)

finished size: tray cloth to fit your tray; napkin, 18in (46cm) square

½yd (0.5m) of 45in (115cm) wide pale floral-print cotton fabric for tray cloth and napkin

¼yd (0.25m) of 18in (46cm) wide fusible web

8in x 5in (18cm x 13cm) piece of green cotton fabric for stem and leaves

7in (18cm) square piece of pink fabric for flower petals

3in (8cm) square piece of yellow fabric for flower centre

Scissors, matching sewing cotton, iron, tracing paper for templates, embroidery hoop (for hand sewing)

EASY LEVEL

FLOWER TRAY CLOTH AND NAPKIN

Set off some pretty china to perfection with a toning tray cloth and napkin set. It would make an ideal gift for Mother's Day or any other special occasion. It is very easy to decorate the set with the hexagonal flower design, which is not pieced together first but applied using a "mock" appliqué method. The trick is to fix the flower in position with a special iron-on bonding material (fusible web) that is available from sewing shops. You can then work around the edges of the motif using a zig-zag machine stitch or alternatively blanket stitch by hand.

1 Measure your tray, then cut a rectangle of the floral-print cotton fabric to the same size plus ¾in (2cm) all around. Next, hem the rectangle as follows. First fold in ⅜in (10mm) round the raw edge and press. Then fold in another ⅜in (1cm) and press. Unfold the edges so you can turn in the corners and press crease line (*see Fig. A*). Cut off the last ⅜in (1cm) of the corner as shown in Fig. B. Double fold the hem again on the pressed lines, mitring the corners, pin and sew as close to the folded edge as you can (*see Fig. C*).

2 Cut a piece of fusible web so that it measures 6in x 4in (15cm x 10cm) in size and apply it paper side up to the wrong side of

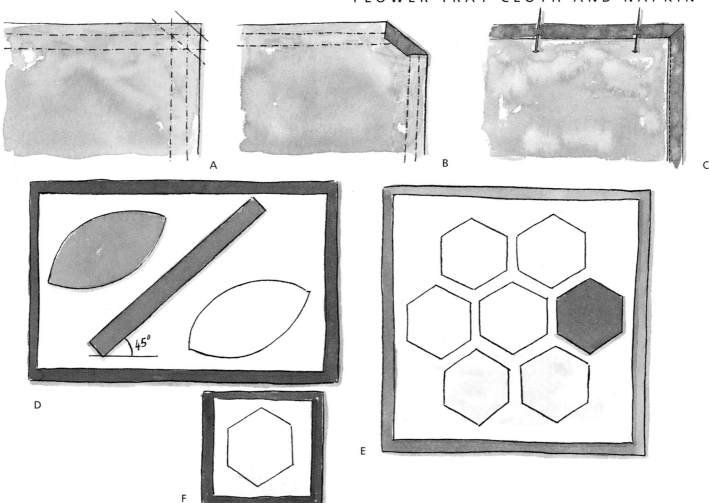

the piece of green fabric, using an iron that is set to the wool setting. It is important that the piece of web is slightly smaller all around than the fabric, otherwise you may find that you get some of the adhesive sticking to the ironing table. Now, with the tracing paper, copy templates on pages 108–109, cut out, then trace a stem (on the bias) and two leaves onto the backing paper (see Fig. D) and cut out the shapes along the lines. Peel away the paper backing and lay the stem and the leaves in the middle of the hemmed tray cloth, placing the stem in a curved shape. Make sure that you leave enough room above it so that you can fit in the large flower. Iron them firmly to the cloth.

3 Cut two pieces of fusible web, one that measures 6in x 6in (15cm x 15cm) and another piece about 2½in x 2½in (5cm x 5cm) in size. Iron the bigger piece to the back of the pink fabric and the smaller piece to the back of the yellow fabric. Copy the hexagon shape onto tracing paper. Cut out and trace onto the paper side of the pink fabric seven times (see Fig. E); transfer one onto the yellow (see Fig. F). Cut out all the hexagons (keeping one pink one back to make the napkin) and remove all of the paper backing. First, iron the yellow middle into position at the top of the stem. Next, place the petals around the middle so that they all touch, and then iron them firmly into position.

4 Neaten the raw edges of the flower motif as follows. If your sewing machine can do zig-zag stitch, set the stitch length to about two and the stitch width to about three. Put some sewing cotton to match the tray cloth in the bobbin, and to match the leaves and stems in the needle. Zig-zag all around the leaves and stem with the middle of the presser foot right on the edge of the design. Change the thread in the needle to match the colour of the flower and then zig-zag all around the middle and the six petals. To sew on the flower by hand, stretch the fabric in an embroidery hoop and work blanket stitch around all parts of the design.

5 To make the napkin, cut out a 19½in (50cm) square from the floral-print cotton fabric left over from making the tray cloth and hem all around it in the same way. Finally, decorate the napkin with a pink hexagon petal and embroider around it as in Step 4.

MATERIALS

finished size: 21½in (55cm) square

1 fat quarter (*see p. 8*) each of turquoise, deep-crimson and black cotton fabrics
1 fat eighth of purple cotton fabric (*see p. 8*)
Rotary cutter (*see pp. 10–11*)
Quilter's ruler
Cutting mat
Matching sewing cotton
Steam iron
22in (60cm) square piece of 2oz (50g) wadding
Quilting materials and design (*see pp. 16–17*)
Small drinking glass
Masking tape, silver pencil
Deep-crimson and turquoise quilting threads
Picture frame with glass

QUILTED AMISH PICTURE

The Amish people are a deeply religious sect who fled persecution in their native Switzerland in the eighteenth century to settle in the northeastern United States. As a group, they are very conservative, shunning all the trappings of modern society. They are well known for their skill at many crafts, and especially for their beautiful patchwork and hand-quilting.

The quilted picture featured here is typical of traditional Amish style. In the past, Amish quiltmakers chose the same rich and sombre colours for their needlework creations as they used for their own clothing. Their religion forbade the use of white, yellow or pastel colours. However, the Amish people today no longer adhere to these strict design rules. Although they still have a reputation for fine craftsmanship, they now make quilts for the tourist trade in the same printed calicos that other quilt-makers use.

The patchwork pattern used for the picture in this project is a miniature version of a traditional central medallion diamond design, with the typical "interrupted" corners, and it is square like almost all Amish designs. The same pattern could easily be adapted to make an attractive quilt for a double bed.

You can vary the colours in the picture if you like, but in general try and keep to the cool side of the colour wheel. You may introduce shades of gray as well as colours like magenta, fuchsia or wine, but do not include any tones of yellow or brown, nor any pastel colours.

1 Cut an 8in (20cm) square of turquoise fabric, four strips of purple 1½in (4cm) wide and 8in (20cm) long, and four 1½in (4cm) squares of deep crimson.

2 Sew two purple strips to each side of turquoise square with ¼in (6mm) seams. Sew deep-crimson squares to each end of other two purple strips. Sew to top and bottom of the larger square, matching seams (*see Fig. A*). Press seams with a steam iron toward the purple strips.

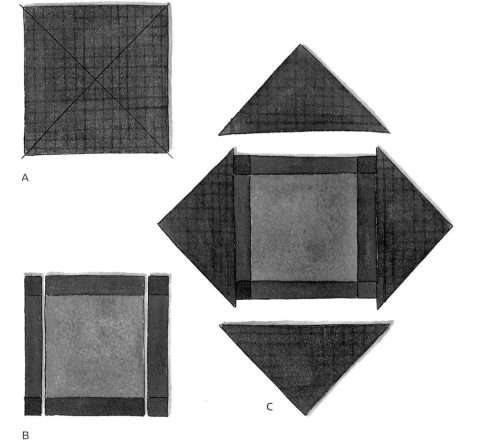

A

B

C

D

3 From black fabric cut an 11in (28cm) square. Fold in both directions diagonally (see Fig. B). Cut on fold lines to make four triangles. Sew triangles to top and bottom of the square (see Fig. C). Press seams toward the purple strips. Then sew other two triangles to each side of the square. Press. Trim square so that the edges are ¼in (6mm) away from deep-crimson corners of inner square. Make sure that you cut it straight.

4 Cut four strips from turquoise fabric 2in (5cm) wide and about 13½in (35cm) long, or exactly the width of the black square. Cut four 2in (5cm) black squares. Sew on strips as in Step 2, taking care not to blunt the deep-crimson corners as you sew (see Fig. D).

5 Cut four strips from deep-crimson fabric 3½in (9cm) wide and about 16½in (42cm) long, or the width of the patchwork square. Cut four 3½in (9cm) black squares. Sew on strips as in Step 2. Press well.

6 Secure patchwork to wadding with a grid of tacking lines about 4in (10cm) apart (see pp. 18–19). Transfer quilting design (see pp. 16–17) to middle using the "prick and pounce" method (see p. 16), joining pounced dots with a silver pencil. Draw interlocking circle pattern in the corners using a small drinking glass. The diagonal pattern on the black triangles is worked along straight lines. Mark these with masking tape, using the photograph as a guide. Quilt by hand, using deep-crimson quilting thread on the turquoise patchwork and turquoise quilting thread on other colours.

7 To finish the picture, mount the patchwork panel in a glazed picture frame and hang on the wall.

MATERIALS

finished size: 25in x 39in (64cm x 99cm)

8 fat eighths (*see p. 8*) of cotton plaids in reds, browns, greens and blue-grays, half in dark tones and half in light

1 fat eighth of plain blue cotton fabric

¼yd (0.25m) of green cotton plaid

½yd (0.5m) of red cotton plaid

¾yd (0.7m) of toning cotton backing fabric

Rotary cutter (*see pp. 10–11*)

Quilter's ruler, cutting mat, steam iron

Two bulldog clips

Matching sewing cotton

1 Pre-wash fabric. From each fat eighth cut seven strips 1¼in (3.5cm) wide and 11in (28cm) long. Separate into darks and lights and hold the bunches together with bulldog clips. From the plain blue fabric, cut out eight tiny 1½in (4cm) squares.

2 Chop off a piece from light bunch and place it right sides together with one tiny blue square. Match up raw edges, pin and sew along one side (*see Fig. A*). Use ¼in (6mm) seams unless otherwise noted. Press the seam away from the blue square.

3 Cut next log at random from bunch of light strips and chop so that it covers first two pieces (*see Fig. B*). Pin and sew on as detailed in Step 2.

4 Chopping the next two logs from the dark-coloured strips, continue sewing on logs in a clockwise direction (*see figs. C and D*). With a ruler, check that logs are sewn parallel to one another. Then alternate two lights and two darks to make a Log Cabin block of four rows (*see Fig. E*).

5 Make up eight Log Cabin blocks that are about 7½in (19cm) square.

6 Arrange blocks with darker halves together to form two large diamonds. Place blocks so that different fabrics are adjacent. When satisfied, sew blocks together. First sew two rows of four blocks, then sew rows together, matching seams. Press seams between blocks open, and press patchwork well from front.

7 Make narrow border. From plain blue fabric, cut six strips 1in (2.5cm) wide and about 18in (46cm) long. Cut two strips to patchwork width and sew to each end. Join other strips to make two long strips. Cut them to patchwork length and sew to each long side (see Fig. F). Press seams away from Log Cabin blocks.

8 Now make second border. From green plaid, cut three strips 2in (5cm) wide and about 44in (115cm) long. Cut one strip into two pieces to patchwork width and sew to each end. Cut long strips to patchwork length and sew to each long side. Press seams outward toward wider border.

9 Finally, make wide border. Cut three strips along the red plaid's length 4½in (11.5cm) wide, or to a width determined by its pattern repeat. Sew on as in Step 8. Press seams toward second border. Press patchwork from front.

10 Cut some toning fabric for the back to patchwork size. Pin two pieces right sides together. Using a ½in (1.5cm) seam, sew around the runner, leaving an 8in (20cm) opening. Clip corners, turn right side out through gap, and press. Sew up opening by hand and press.

HOMESPUN LOG CABIN RUNNER

Instead of using a conventional cloth, try decorating your table with this unusual Log Cabin runner made in plaid and striped fabrics. Unlike a tablecloth, it will not hide an attractive piece of furniture, yet it still protects the surface of your table. The patchwork is made up of eight Log Cabin blocks, arranged in a diamond pattern. If you wish, you can form all sorts of other interesting patterns such as pinwheels and chevrons by simply rotating the blocks (see Fig. F). You can also vary the width of the border to make your runner a different size. If you enjoy the Log Cabin technique, why not add more blocks to create a stunning wall hanging? The fabrics specified are all 45in (115cm) wide unless otherwise stated.

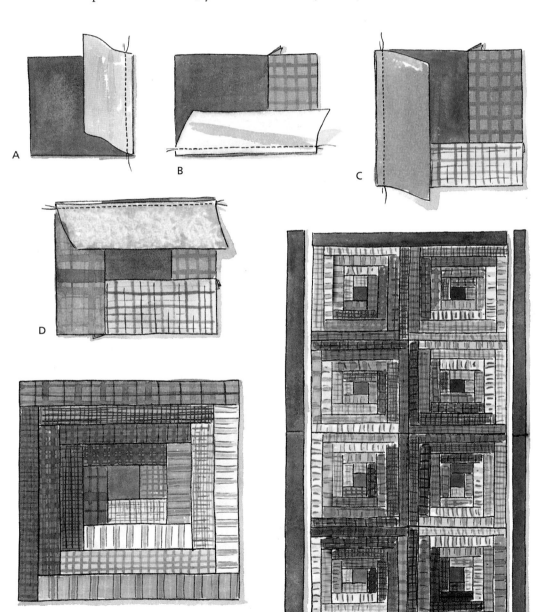

A

B

C

D

E

F

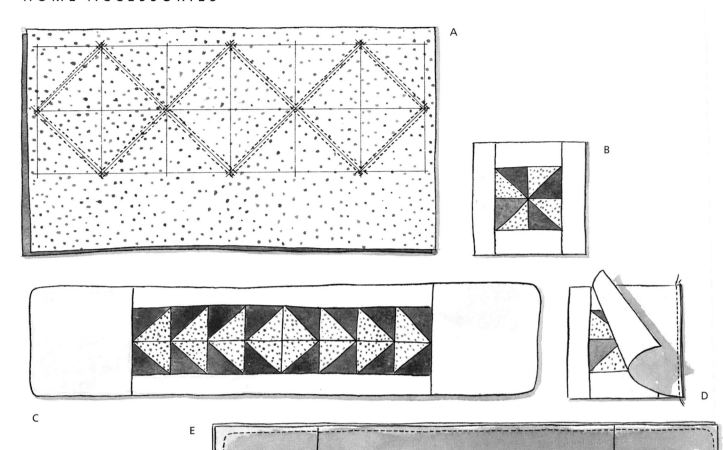

A

B

C

D

E

MATERIALS

finished size: 7in x 30in (18cm x76cm)

1 fat eighth (*see p. 8*) each of light geometric print and dark-green floral print cotton fabric

⅜yd (0.35m) of light floral print cotton fabric for front

¼yd (0.25m) of dark-green print cotton fabric for lining

No.2 template from 2-inch set of R.I.T. Squares (*see pp. 12–13*)

Ballpoint pen, rotary cutter (*see pp. 10–11*)

Quilter's ruler, cutting mat

Matching sewing cotton

Steam iron

2 7in (18cm) square pieces of mediumweight iron-on interfacing

7in x 30in (18cm x 76cm) strip of cotton bump (heavy curtain interlining)

1 To make the patchwork for the pinwheel blocks and "flying geese" border, place the light geometric print and the dark-green floral print fabric right sides together. Using the No.2 R.I.T. Square template as a guide, draw a grid of 12 squares on the back of one of the pieces (*see Fig. A*). Sew and cut (*see pp. 12–13*) to make up 24 No.2 patches. All seams are ¼in (6mm) unless otherwise noted.

2 Make two pinwheel blocks as follows. For each pinwheel, lay out four No.2 patches to match Fig. B. Sew patches together to make two rows, and then sew rows together, matching up seams. Press with a steam iron.

3 Then make "flying geese" border. Sew No.2 patches together in pairs to make the "geese" and then sew the geese together (*see Fig. C*). Press, straightening out the border against a line drawn onto your ironing table.

4 From light floral print fabric, cut three strips 1¾in (4.5cm) wide and 44in (115cm) long. Also cut four 7in (18cm) squares from one long strip. Cut two strips to the same length as the flying geese border and sew to each side. Press

seams outward. Sew a 7in (18cm) square to each end of the border (*see Fig. C*). Cut four strips to the width of the two pinwheel blocks and sew to top and bottom. Press the seams outward. Cut four more strips to the blocks' length and sew to each side (*see Fig. B*). Then press the seams outward.

5 Apply a square of iron-on interfacing to back of pinwheel blocks. To face blocks, place on remaining two light floral print squares with right sides together, and sew along one side (*see Fig. D*). Press right sides out. Tack the pinwheel squares face up to the ends of the oven glove,

matching all raw edges. Trim the excess material along the oven glove to make same width as pinwheel squares.

6 Assemble the oven glove. Place the bump on the wrong side of the dark-green print lining fabric and then trim to the same length. Pin together. Pin lining to the patchwork right sides together. Sew all the way around the oven glove, rounding off the corners and leaving a gap of 4in (10cm) (*see Fig. E*). Trim the bump close to the seam line, clip the corners, and then turn the oven glove right side out. Hand-stitch up the opening to finish.

FLORAL OVEN GLOVE

Easy to make in floral prints, this oven glove would be a lovely household present for someone. You need the 2-inch set of R.I.T. Squares for this project. Simple half-square triangles are combined to create the "flying geese" border and the pinwheels at each end. Choose a dark lining colour, as the glove shows the dirt. If you can't find cotton bump for padding, use towelling or two layers of winceyette. Synthetic wadding won't protect against hot pans. All the fabric specified is 45in (115cm) wide unless otherwise stated.

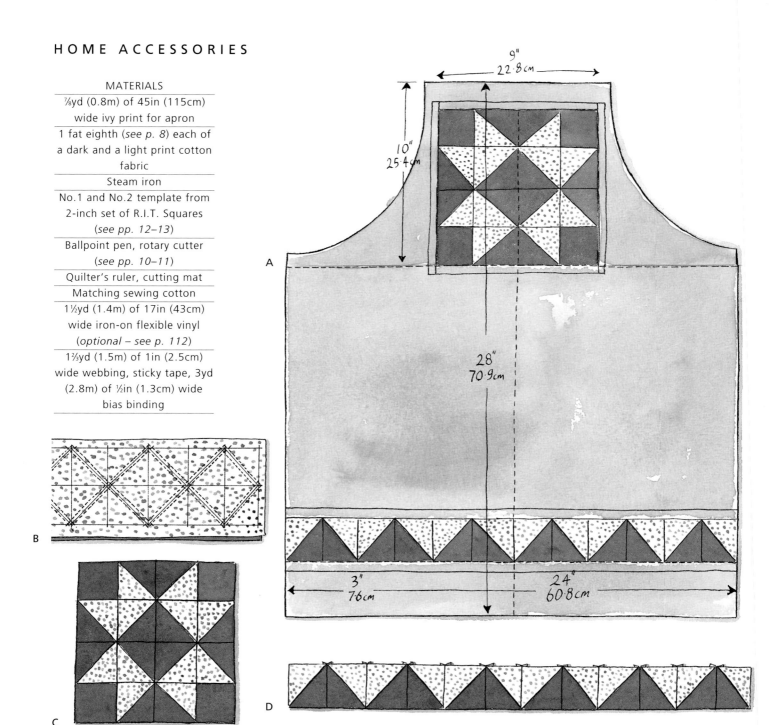

INTERMEDIATE LEVEL

IVY APRON

This simple butcher-style apron has a block known as "Variable Star" on the bib and a zig-zag border along the hem. The 2-inch set of R.I.T. Squares is used for the patchwork. With this set, each patch in a block or border measures 2in (5cm) square when assembled, so the 16-patch Variable Star block illustrated finishes at 8in (20cm) square – just the right size for decorating a clothing item or a small patchwork project. The ivy print cotton fabric illustrated makes an attractive background for the patchwork. If you prefer, use a heavier-weight cotton fabric such as butcher's stripe, furnishing fabric or canvas. To protect your apron, a special iron-on vinyl covering is available.

1 Scale up pattern (*see Fig. A*) and cut out apron from ivy print fabric. No seam allowance is needed as raw edge will be bound. Press fold lines with steam iron to help place patchwork.

2 Place dark-print and light-print fabric right sides together. Using No.2 R.I.T. Square template as a guide, draw a grid

88

of 12 squares on the back of one of the pieces (*see Fig. B*). Sew, cut and press (*see pp. 12–13*) to make 24 No.2 patches. All seams are ¼in (6mm) unless otherwise noted. Using No.1 template, cut four 2½in (6.5cm) squares from darker print fabric.

3 To assemble 16-patch block, lay out 12 of the No.2 patches and the four No.1 patches as in Fig. C. Sew patches together to make four rows, then sew rows together, matching seams. Press. Cut a strip 1in (2.5cm) wide across width of ivy print fabric. From this, cut two strips to the block's width and sew to each side. Cut two more strips to block's length and sew to top and bottom. Turn under a ¼in (6mm) hem all around block and press. Pin block centrally on apron and in line with pressed line. Machine sew close to folded edge.

4 To make patchwork border, lay out remaining No.2 patches according to Fig. D and sew together. Press seams open and block border so it is straight. Cut two strips from ivy print fabric as in Step 3 to the same length as the border and sew to each side. Turn under a hem along border and apply it to the apron along pressed line, as above. If preferred, apply iron-on flexible vinyl to the apron, following the manufacturer's instructions carefully.

5 From webbing, cut a neck strap 24in (60cm) and two ties 18in (45cm) long. Hold strap and ties in place with sticky tape on the back of apron to keep the ends of the webbing in line with apron's raw edges. Sew on binding all way around apron, catching in neck strap and ties. Remove sticky tape, and turn straps and ties outward. Stitch about ⅛in (3mm) away from edge of the binding to hold straps and ties in position.

INTERMEDIATE LEVEL

MARMALADE CAT

Cat lovers young and old will adore this cheeky ginger patchwork cat. The ideal pet, he won't leave hairs all over your furniture, nor sit on your newspaper when you are trying to read it!

The cat is made up in "strippy" patchwork in a variety of marmalade-coloured prints, and its features are embroidered on. You could also use the same simple technique to make a child a cuddly teddy, an Easter bunny or a dog, perhaps. Look in the pattern books at your local dress fabric shop to get other ideas for making different types of stuffed animals.

A

90

MATERIALS

finished size: 14in (36cm) tall

1 fat quarter (*see p. 8*) in each of four marmalade-coloured print cotton fabrics

Steam iron, rotary cutter (*see pp. 10–11*), quilter's ruler, cutting mat

Matching sewing cotton, ⅝yd (0.6m) of mediumweight iron-on interfacing

Photocopied pattern, water-erasable pen, blunt instrument

Black embroidery cotton

8oz (200g) polyester toy filling

Ribbon and bell to decorate

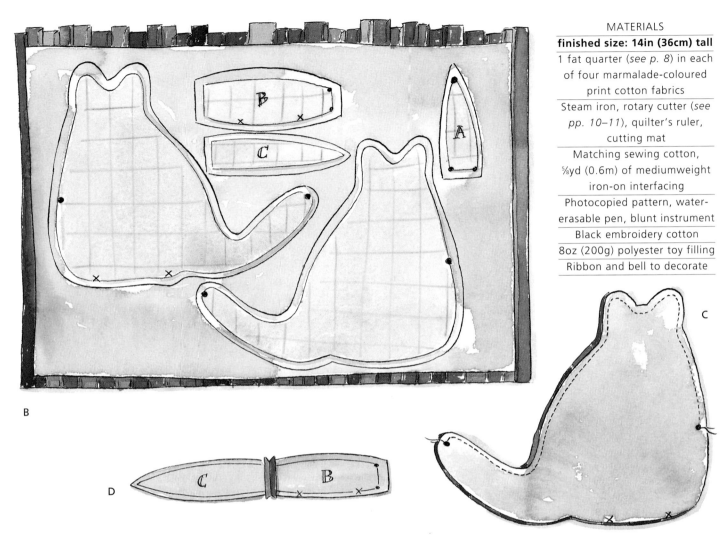

1 **Press the four fat quarters** together with a steam iron and cut through all layers at once with rotary cutter to make eight strips from each fabric 1½in (4cm) wide and about 22in (56cm) long.

2 **Arranging the 32 strips in** random order so that no two identical fabrics are adjacent, sew them together to make a "strippy" sheet (*see Fig. A*) about 22in x 32in (56cm x 81cm). Use ¼in (6mm) seams throughout. Press seams to one side.

3 **Cut out a piece of iron-on** interfacing that is slightly smaller in size all round than the strippy sheet and then iron it to the wrong side of the patchwork so that you reinforce it.

4 **Enlarge the pattern pieces for** the cat by 165% (*see pp. 108–109*) using a photocopier. Trace them onto the wrong (interfacing) side of the patchwork, leaving at least ½in (12mm) between the pieces for seam allowances. The traced line will be your sewing line. Mark the large and small dots and stars (*see Fig. B*). Cut out the pieces adding a ¼in (6mm) seam allowance all round.

5 **To transfer the cat's face to the** patchwork, pin or tape the design under the cat's head and then place the patchwork against a window. Copy the features with a water-erasable pen, then embroider by hand or satin-stitch by machine with some black embroidery cotton.

6 **Place the cat front and cat** back right sides together. Stitch round the body on the sewing lines from the large dot on the front of the cat, over the ears to the dot that is at the tip of its tail (*see Fig. C*). Clip the seams at the large dots. Then with right sides together, sew the front gusset (A in Fig. A) to the body from the small dots at the base to the large dot placed below the chin. Sew the tail gusset (C) to the base of the body (B) (*see Fig. D*).

7 **Cut extra pieces of interlining** and iron in place on the front and back of the ears and on the base to reinforce them. Sew the base and tail to the cat's body, matching the dots. Leave a gap between "star" symbols.

8 **Clip the seams to the sewing** lines and trim closely around the ears and the end of the tail. Turn the cat so that it is right side out and, using a blunt pointed instrument, carefully push out the ears and the end of the tail. Stuff as firmly as possible with the polyester toy filling and then sew up the gap. To finish, decorate your marmalade cat with a pretty ribbon tied in a bow and a bell.

MATERIALS

(to make one mat and napkin set)

finished size: mat, 17in x 11½in (43cm x 30cm); napkin, 18in (46cm) square

Scraps of cotton fabric in range of blue tones

½yd (0.5m) of 45in (115cm) wide maroon print cotton fabric

1 sheet of white paper for templates

Greaseproof paper and 1 sheet of mediumweight white paper for foundations

Clear adhesive tape or spray adhesive

Scissors

Table lamp

Steam iron

12in x 18in (30cm x 45cm) piece of 2oz (50g) polyester wadding

⅔yd (0.6m) of 17in (43cm) iron-on flexible vinyl *(optional – see p.112)*

1⅔yd (1.5m) of ½in (1.3cm) wide navy blue bias binding

Sewing cotton in maroon and navy blue

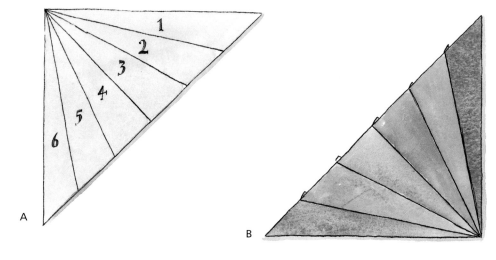

A

B

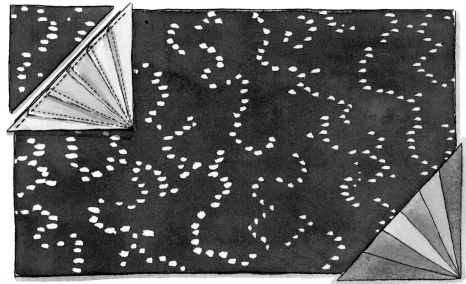

C

1 Scale up foundation design in Fig. A to 265% on white paper or enlarge on a photocopier. Trace two copies onto greaseproof paper and one onto white, numbering each area.

2 Cut out six templates from the white paper and stick them on wrong side of the blue fabric scraps using rolled-up adhesive tape. Cut round templates with a margin of ⅜in (1cm).

3 Remove template from Piece 1. Place it right side out on blank side of transparent paper foundation. Use your table lamp

to check that it covers Area 1 and pin it in place.

4 Take Piece 2 and using your lamp to check its position, place it right side over Piece 1 so that the the paper template's edge is on the line between Areas 1 and 2. Remove template and pin Piece 2 in position. On the other side, machine stitch on the line between 1 and 2.

5 Remove pin and fold Piece 2 over to cover Area 2. Check with light that it is correctly positioned. Then fold Piece 2 back over Piece 1 again and trim seam

(less than ¼in [6mm]) to sewing line. Fold Piece 2 back over Area 2 and press with a steam iron.

6 Repeat Steps 4 and 5 with other four blue fabric pieces so that the foundation block forms a triangle (*see Fig. B*). Machine stitch around block, just outside the drawn line. Make another foundation block in the same way.

7 From maroon-print fabric, cut a rectangle 17in x 11½in (43cm x 30cm). Place a foundation block right side down adjacent to the upper left-hand corner of the mat (*see Fig. C*), making sure it is

positioned squarely to the corner. Sew right across the corner on the line as shown.

8 Tear away foundation, dampening a bit first. Trim off corner of maroon print fabric about ¼in (6mm) away from seam (*see Fig. C*). Sew other block to opposite corner in the same way. Press the seams of the corner triangles outward.

9 From maroon print fabric, cut a placemat back, just slightly larger than the front. Cut some wadding to match. Make a quilt sandwich (*see pp. 18–19*) and quilt

in a pleasing all-over pattern by hand or by machine. If preferred, apply some iron-on flexible vinyl to both sides of the place mat, following the manufacturer's instructions. Finally, round off the mat's corners by tracing them around a large teacup, and trimming away any excess wadding. Bind the place mat with bias binding.

10 For the matching napkin, cut a 19½in (50cm) square from maroon-print fabric. Turn under a double ⅜in (10mm) hem, mitring the corners, and then sew by hand or machine. Make other sets that are needed in the same way.

INTERMEDIATE LEVEL

BREAKFAST SET

Everyone needs place mats in their home, and this one with its attractive patchwork corner motif and a matching napkin is ideal to use at breakfast time on the table or at the breakfast bar. The set will also fit on a tray so that breakfast can be served to someone who is still in bed.

The corner motifs shown are made from a fabric printed with "bars" of different tones of blue. However, you could use as many different printed or plain pieces of cotton fabric from your scrap bag as you like, as long as they go well with the fabric you have chosen for the mats.

The technique used for this project is foundation piecing (*see pp. 14–15*), which makes easy work of the odd-shaped triangles that are included in the motif. The paper foundation, which can be any lightweight transparent paper such as greaseproof paper, can simply be torn away afterwards.

Make several of the sets and use them for a dinner party or for when people come to afternoon tea. To make the place mat easy to wipe clean after each meal, apply iron-on flexible vinyl to both sides before sewing on the final binding.

For convenience, set up your work table with a table lamp and a steam iron before you begin making the patchwork.

93

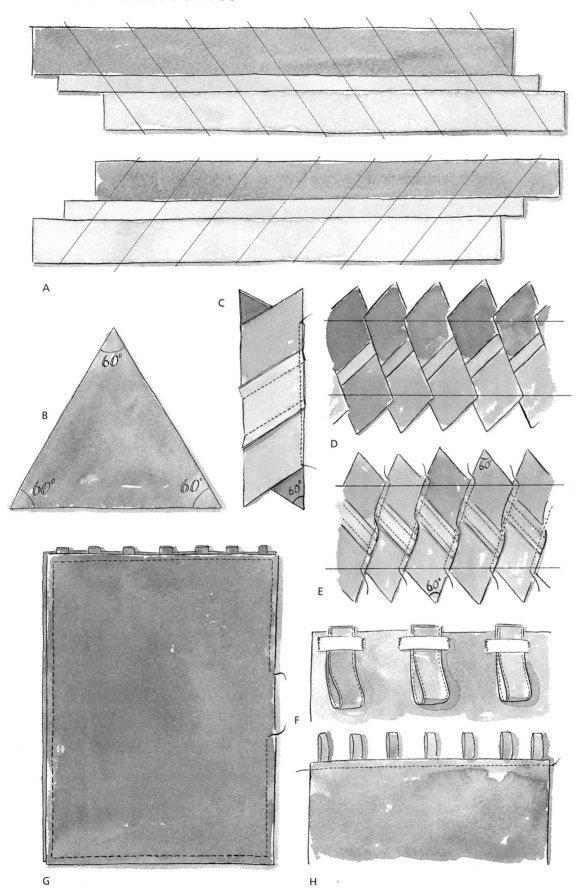

A

B

C

D

E

F

G

H

MATERIALS

¼yd (0.25m) each of yellow print, plain pink, pale-green print and mid-green print cotton fabrics
Length of yellow print cotton fabric for two panels to fit your window plus loops
Lining fabric to match
Rotary cutter (see pp. 10–11)
Quilter's ruler
Cutting mat
White paper
Matching sewing cotton
Steam iron
Clear adhesive tape
Large safety pin or bodkin

1 To make two mirror-image Seminole bands up to 30in (76cm) long each, cut strips about 44in (112cm) long as follows: two strips of yellow-print fabric 2¾in (7cm) wide; two strips of plain pink 1in (2.5cm) wide; one strip each of mid-green print and pale-green print, 2¾in (7cm) wide. Cut strips in half to 22in (56cm) long.

2 Sew strips together (see Fig. A) for four strip sets, two with mid-green and two with pale-green fabric. Stagger one mid-green set and one pale-green set to left and the other two sets to right. All seams are ¼in (6mm) unless otherwise noted. Press seams away from pink stripe with a steam iron. With quilter's ruler and rotary cutter cut strip sets at a 60° angle and 2½in (6.5cm) wide (see Fig. A). Cut two strip sets angled toward the right and two toward the left (see Fig. A). Keep separate. Cut about seven pieces from each strip set.

3 Trace triangular template (see Fig. B) onto white paper. Using template as a guide to place pieces correctly, sew together as follows, making sure the yellow fabric is upward, and alternating a piece containing mid-green with one containing pale-green. Fix template with some rolled-up adhesive tape to top right side of one piece (*see Fig. C*). Place next piece on top right sides together so it is in line with template. Continue sewing each next piece until you have sewn two mirror-image bands (*see Fig. D*). Press seams in two directions as Fig.E.

4 Trim triangular ends from pieces (*see Fig. E*).The two mirror-image bands are about 4in (10cm) wide. Cut two strips each of mid-green and pink fabrics, 1in (2.5cm) wide and to each curtain panel's width plus 1in (2.5cm). Sew a mid-green strip to top and a pink strip to bottom of each band – try not to stretch as you sew. Press and block each band (*see p. 18*). Cut a strip 2½in (6.5cm) wide from each curtain panel. Sew to bottom of each band. Sew bands to bottom of curtain panels. Press. Cut both panels to length plus 1in (2cm); cut lining pieces to same size.

5 Next, make hanging loops. The loops are about 5in (12cm) apart, so for two panels 30in (75cm) wide you need 14 loops. From yellow print fabric, cut strips 2½in (6.5cm) wide. Fold lengthways and sew ¼in (6mm) away from raw edges. Use safety pin or bodkin to turn them right sides out, and press. Stitch around edge on each side, cut the pieces 4½in (11cm) long. Hold loops in place with adhesive tape along top of curtain panel, matching raw edges (*see Fig. F*). Make sure loops are same length before sewing in.

6 Pin lining to panel, right sides together. Sew with ½in (1.3cm) seam all around, leaving gap on one side, as Fig. G. Turn curtains right way out through gap and slip-stitch by hand. Press. Top stitch at top edge of curtain to reinforce loops (*see Fig. H*). Repeat for second curtain.

SEMINOLE CURTAINS

These unusual curtains, with their border of Seminole patchwork, are a marriage of two different cultures. The idea for the curtains came from Japan, where panels of fabric are suspended from poles with loops and used instead of doors to separate tiny rooms in houses and flats; the sewing technique is American. These curtains are designed for a window, so that when the light shines through, the seams in the Seminole bands are shown up, emphasizing the intricacy of the design. The fabrics used are pastel cotton prints, which you can coordinate with your room colours. For each curtain, you need enough fabric to cut two panels half the width of your window and the length of your window plus 1in (2.5cm) all round. You also need ¼yd (0.25m) extra to make loops. The fabric quantities detailed are sufficient for two 30in (76cm) borders, and all fabrics specified are 45in (115cm) wide.

SEMINOLE PINCUSHIONS

These bright pincushions are ideal to hold all your spare pins. They are created from remnants of the patchwork bands used for the Seminole Cushion (*see pp. 58–59*) or the Christmas Stocking (*see pp. 106–107*), so if you decide to try those projects, why not sew the pincushions as well?

Alternatively, you can make up the Seminole bands using the fabric quantities as given for the cushion bands. One patchwork length can make as many as eight pincushions, and as it only takes a few minutes to sew each one, you will soon have several that you can give to friends as gifts for special occasions.

Seminole patchwork is fascinating to stitch, and the small scale of the work lends itself to projects such as the pincushions. You start with narrow strips of brightly coloured fabric which you sew together to make what are known as "strip sets". These are then cut into small pieces, sometimes at an angle. Depending on how you sew the pieces together again, you can create wonderful designs for geometric borders.

As the strips for Seminole patchwork are often cut as narrow as ¾in (2cm) in width, only tiny patches of certain colours will be visible in the finished design after seaming.

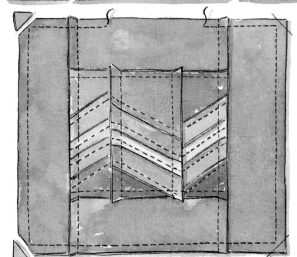

A

B

MATERIALS

(to make one or several pincushions)

Small remnant or remnants of Seminole patchwork 2in (5cm) to 3in (8cm) long

Scissors, scraps of two or three toning plain cotton fabrics for borders and backs, matching sewing cotton

1 bag of polyester toy filling

Long needle, contrasting embroidery sewing cotton

1 Square off a remnant of Seminole patchwork to make it symmetrical. Alternatively, make up one or more of the Seminole bands described on page 58.

2 Cut strips of toning fabric between 1in (2.5cm) and 1½in (4cm) wide. Sew strips to patchwork, first to top and bottom, then to each side (*see Fig. A*). If you wish, sew on a second border all round to enlarge the pincushion. The finished size can be between 3in (8cm) and 5in (12cm).

3 If you have fancy stitches on your sewing machine, you can embellish the patchwork by stitching across the bands or all around the borders.

4 Cut a piece of plain fabric for the back to the same size as the front. With right sides together, sew around the four sides, ¼in (6mm) away from the raw edges, leaving a gap for the stuffing (*see Fig. B*). Clip off the corners and turn through to the right side.

5 Stuff as full as possible with toy filling, and sew up the gap by hand. If your pincushion is larger than about 3½in (9cm) long, it is best to tie down the middle, otherwise you might lose your needles in the filling. Thread a long needle with four strands of embroidery cotton and make a long double loop down through the middle and back up through the same point. Tie threads in a double knot, then trim ends to ¾in (2cm).

6 Make tassels for the corners of the chevron pincushion in the same way, binding them several times at the base. If you are making several pincushions, make the remainder using the same method as above.

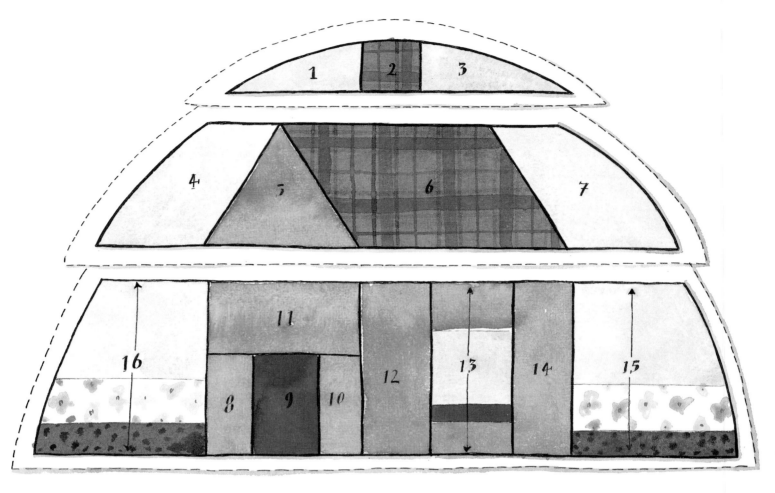

MATERIALS

finished size: 7in x 13½in (18cm x 34cm)

Cotton scraps for "cottage" foundation block: blue for sky and window; light-yellow and mid-yellow prints for walls; red print for door and windowsill; dark-green print for grass; floral print for garden; lace for curtain

1 fat quarter (*see p. 8*) of brown plaid cotton fabric for roof and cosy back, 1 fat quarter of toning lining fabric

Photocopied design, greaseproof paper for foundation, scissors, clear adhesive tape, matching sewing thread, steam iron

15in x 24in (40cm x 60cm) piece of 4oz (100g) wadding, 1yd (0.9m) of 1in (2.5cm) gray bias binding, button for doorknob

1 Scale up above pattern to 182% onto white paper or enlarge it on a photocopier. This design fits a standard four-cup teapot. If your teapot needs a bigger cosy, just draw or photocopy the "dome" shape to the required size and scale up the cottage to fit. Trace the design from your photocopy onto greaseproof paper. Be sure to number each area and make a note of which colour fabric will cover it. Cut your photocopy into template pieces on the heavy lines, cutting Pieces 13, 15 and 16 as one piece. Cut the greaseproof foundation into three parts on the dotted lines.

2 Using rolled-up adhesive tape, stick the back of the templates to the right sides of the appropriate

fabrics. Cut out fabric around the templates, leaving a margin of ½in (1.3cm) all around. Leave templates in place until you need the pieces. (Stick on the templates of Pieces 13, 15 and 16 at Steps 4 and 5.)

3 Sew together the three pieces of Part I and then the four pieces of Part II following the instructions for Foundation Piecing on pages 14–15. Press pieces in place with a steam iron and sew around the perimeter, but do not remove the paper foundations yet.

4 Part III is more complicated because you need to pre-piece Areas 13, 15 and 16 before they are pieced to the foundation paper. (All pre-pieced bits are sewn together with ¼in [6mm] seams.) To make Area 13 (the window),

cut a 2in (5cm) square of light blue. Sew a tiny ¾in (2cm) wide strip of red print fabric to one side and press. Pin a lace scrap to the window. Sew a 1½in (4cm) wide strip of mid-yellow to the top of the window to hold lace in place. Sew another strip of mid-yellow 1in (2.5cm) wide to below the windowsill. Press. Stick template 13 to the back of the whole piece. Now sew Area 13 to Area 12 in the usual way. Sew on Area 14.

5 To make Areas 15 and 16, cut three strips about 8in (20cm) long: light blue 2¼in (6cm) wide; light floral print 1½in (4cm) wide; and dark-green print 1¼in (3.5cm) wide. Sew together to make a strip-set. Cut in half, stick on appropriate template 15 or 16 and sew remaining pieces to the foundation.

Stitch around the whole of Part III to hold the pieces in place and then press. Sew Parts I, II and III together on the sewing lines, taking care that you match up the roof's corners accurately with the sides of the house.

6 Cut a strip of dark-green print fabric that is about 14in (35cm) long and 2in (5cm) wide. Sew the strip below the house and press well. Tear away all of the paper foundation, dampening it first with water.

7 To make the loop for the "chimney", cut out a square of roof fabric that is about 3½in (9cm) x 3½in (9cm). Fold in the raw edges to make a strip about 1in (2.5cm) wide. Stitch along the edges on both sides.

8 From the brown plaid fabric, cut a back to the same size as the cosy front (be sure to include the seam allowance). Cut two pieces for lining, and two pieces of wadding to match. Fold the chimney in half and pin in position upside down on the cottage roof. Lay the cottage block and the back wrong side down on the pieces of wadding and zig-zag around the edges. Place front and back right sides together and sew around dome shape, using a ½in (1.3cm) seam. Sew the two lining pieces together in the same way. Press.

9 Put the lining inside the cosy and then bind around the lower edge with the bias binding to finish. Tack the lining to the inside of the roof and sew on a tiny button for a door handle.

COTTAGE TEA COSY

This tea cosy conjures up the happy times of yesteryear, when families sat around a big scrubbed pine kitchen table listening to the wireless and enjoying endless cups of tea from the big old teapot.

If you enjoy creating pictures with patchwork, you can have fun making this useful kitchen accessory, which is filled with a thick layer of wadding to keep your tea hot in the pot. The same cottage design could be repeated in square blocks to make a delightful cot quilt. Use the foundation piecing method (*see pp. 14–15*), working on a paper foundation, such as greaseproof paper, which can easily be removed when the patchwork is complete.

CHRISTMAS DECORATIONS

Patchwork is an ideal medium for making pretty ornaments to go on the Christmas tree or Christmas cards, as scraps left over from other projects can be put to good use. A Christmas stocking, made from Seminole bands, will also delight young children when they see it hanging full of small presents by the fireplace or at the end of their beds on Christmas morning.

EASY LEVEL

CHECKERBOARD TREE ORNAMENT

Try making this pretty ornament for your Christmas tree. First, sew a patchwork rectangle and make it into a little bag. Then blow up a small balloon inside the bag and paint it with a "stiffy bow" solution to make the bag rigid (*see p. 112 for stockists*). When dry, decorate with ribbon and hang on your Christmas tree.

MATERIALS

finished size: about 4in (10cm) in diameter

1 fat eighth (*see p. 8*) each of blue-green Christmas print and plain dark-green fabric

Rotary cutter (*see pp. 10–11*), quilter's ruler, cutting board

Matching sewing thread, steam iron, small balloon

Bottle of "stiffy bow" solution (*see p. 112*), small paintbrush

Spray varnish, ½yd (0.5m) blue tartan satin ribbon, thick thread

A

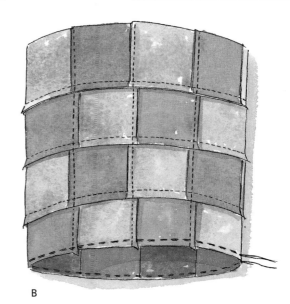

B

1 From each fabric piece cut four strips 1¾in (4.5cm) wide and 7½in (20cm) long. Sew eight strips together to make a small "strippy" sheet. All seams are ¼in (6mm) unless otherwise noted. Press seams to one side with a steam iron. Chop across strippy sheet to make four checkered strips, 1¾in (4.5cm) wide.

2 Turn every other strip around so that checkers are staggered and so that the seams go in opposite directions. Sew strips together (*see Fig. A*). Press seams open.

3 Fold rectangle in half, right sides together, and sew side seam. Sew a line of long gathering stitches around the bottom, ¼in (6mm) from raw edge (*see Fig. B*). Gather up tightly to form a bag and machine-stitch across bottom.

4 Turn bag right side out. By hand, sew a line of gathering stitches around the top with some strong thread about 15in (40cm) long. Place a balloon inside the bag and gather up the top. Bring the neck of the balloon through the opening and tie off the gathered top, leaving a hole the size of your little finger. The ends of the thread will hang the ball.

5 Blow up the balloon inside the bag and tie. Slightly dampen the cloth ball and paint liberally with "stiffy bow" solution. Dry, and apply another coat.

6 When ball is rigid and dry, push the neck of the balloon back inside it and spray with several coats of varnish, drying between coats. Decorate with a satin ribbon bow and tie thread to hang.

PINE TREE CHRISTMAS ORNAMENT

The pine tree band on this pretty Christmas tree ornament is fun to sew using the foundation piecing method (*see pp. 14–15*). The design is pieced onto a paper foundation which is torn away after sewing. For convenience, set up your work table with a lamp and iron before you begin this technique. Follow the easy instructions on page 101 to make up the hollow ball.

MATERIALS
finished size: about 3½in (9cm) in diameter
1 fat eighth (*see p. 8*) each of sky blue, dark-green and white fabrics
Scaling paper
Scissors
White paper for templates
Greaseproof paper for foundation
Matching sewing cotton
Black felt marker, steam iron
Other materials as for Checkerboard tree ornament (*see p. 101*)
½yd (0.5m) blue satin ribbon

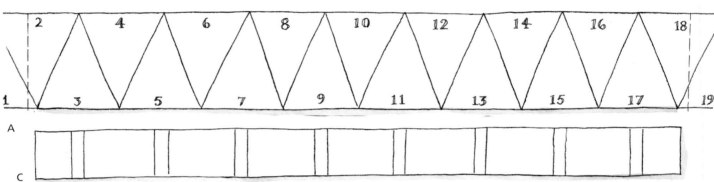

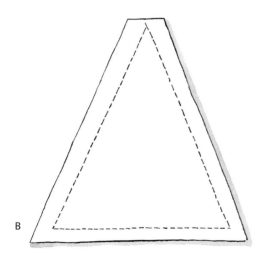

1 Scale up pine tree design by 50% (*see Fig. A*) and trace onto the greaseproof paper. Be sure to number the areas of the design. Use the triangular template (*see Fig. B*) shown here to cut nine sky blue triangular pieces and ten dark green, adding about ⅜in (10mm) seam allowances.

2 Following the instructions for foundation piecing (*see pp. 14–15*), sew the blue and green pieces in correct order to back of the paper foundation. When the foundation strip is complete, trim off excess fabric on either side to ¼in (6mm) from the top and the bottom of trees and on dotted lines.

3 From the sky blue fabric, cut two strips ¾in (2cm) wide and length of row of trees. On one of the strips paint in the tree trunks with a felt marker using Fig. C as a guide. Sew strips to each side of tree strip, on the sewing line, lining up the tree trunks correctly under trees. Press with a steam iron, then dampen and tear away paper foundation. Cut two strips of white fabric 2¼in (6cm) wide and length of tree row. Sew them to the top and bottom of the patchwork strip to form a rectangle, and press. Trim the patchwork on each side to make an even rectangular shape.

4 Join sides of the rectangle by sewing through sky pieces numbered 1 and 17. To make up patchwork ball, follow steps 3 to 6 in the Checkerboard Tree Ornament on page 101, but decorate with blue ribbon.

MATERIALS
finished size: about 4in (10cm) in diameter

1 fat eighth (*see p.8*) each of red, wine, white and dark-green fabrics

Rotary cutter (*see pp. 10–11*), quilter's ruler, cutting board

Other materials as for Checkerboard Tree Ornament (*see p. 101*)

½yd (0.5m) dark-green satin ribbon

ADVANCED LEVEL

SEMINOLE TREE ORNAMENT

To make this attractive Christmas tree ornament, you will need a Seminole band in four different colours. Use off-cuts of fabric from your scrap bag or choose Christmas fabrics in seasonal shades such as the green and red shown here. Ideally only use imperial measurements and follow the instructions in the Checkerboard Tree Ornament (*see p. 101*) to make up the decoration.

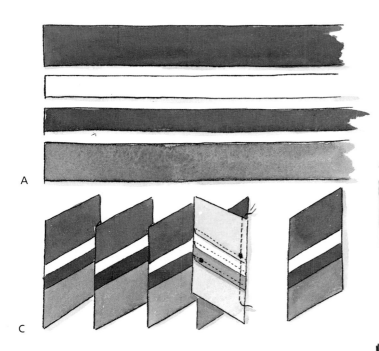

A

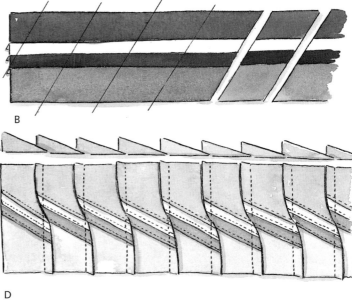

B

D

C

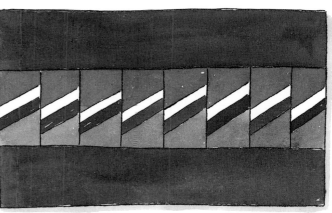

E

1 For zig-zag Seminole band, cut two strips 18in (46cm) long from each colour in these widths: wine 1½in (4cm); white ¾in (2cm); red ¾in (2cm); dark green 1½in (4cm) (*see Fig. A*). Sew together with ¼in (6mm) seams for two strip sets. Press to one side with a steam iron and block-press (*see p. 18*) strips.

2 Cut strip set pieces 1½in (4cm) wide and at a 60° angle (*see Fig. B*). Make two dots on back of pieces ¼in (6mm) in from raw edges,

where seams meet (*see Fig. C*). Sew 11 pieces together, matching dots (*see Fig. C*). Press seams (*see Fig. D*). Trim band (*see Fig. D*) so edges are ¾in (2cm) away from furthest white and red points. Cut two red fabric strips 2¼in (5.5cm) wide. Cut strips and patchwork band 10½in (26.5cm) long and sew strips to band's sides (*see Fig. E*). Press seams toward red strips. To make up the ball, follow Steps 3 to 6 in Checkerboard Tree Ornament on page 101, but decorate with the green ribbon.

SEMINOLE CHRISTMAS CARDS

It is always more personal to send a home-made Christmas card, and your family and friends will be delighted to receive these colourful Seminole designs. When you make Seminole bands for projects such as cushions, pieces are often left over that are ideal for small items like these cards.

The techniques for making the two Seminole cards in the middle and on the right of the photograph are explained in the Seminole Cushion project on pages 58–59, while the instructions for the card on the left can be found in the Seminole Tree Ornament on page 103. From one Seminole band you can make four to six Christmas cards. To make more, follow the instructions to make one of the bands as detailed in the relevant projects and use accordingly.

MATERIALS
(to make four to six cards each of three designs)

Seminole patchwork bands (see pp. 58–59, 103, 106–107)

Scraps of contrasting or matching fabrics, clear adhesive tape, matching sewing cotton

Blank cards with square or round apertures 3in–4in (8cm–10cm) across

1 Use a Seminole band (*see figs. A, B and C*) that is approximately square in shape. If making more cards, first make a Seminole band following the instructions in the appropriate project. Sew strips of matching or contrasting fabric to the piece so that the finished bit of patchwork is marginally larger than the opening in the card. Finally, tape the patchwork to the inside of the cutout.

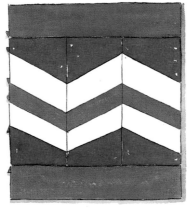

A

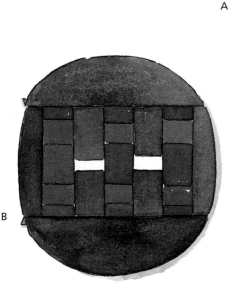

B

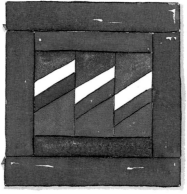

C

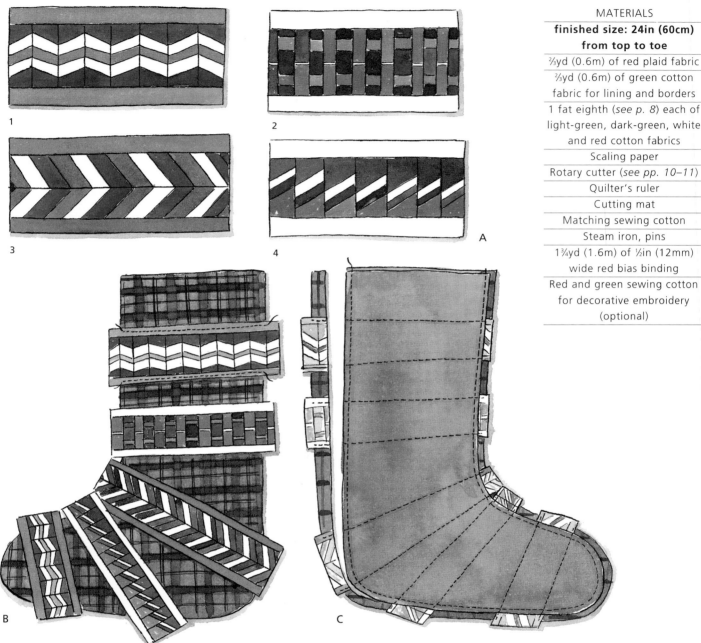

1

2

3

4

A

B

C

finished size: 24in (60cm)
from top to toe
⅔yd (0.6m) of red plaid fabric
⅔yd (0.6m) of green cotton fabric for lining and borders
1 fat eighth (*see p. 8*) each of light-green, dark-green, white and red cotton fabrics
Scaling paper
Rotary cutter (*see pp. 10–11*)
Quilter's ruler
Cutting mat
Matching sewing cotton
Steam iron, pins
1¾yd (1.6m) of ½in (12mm) wide red bias binding
Red and green sewing cotton for decorative embroidery (optional)

ADVANCED LEVEL

CHRISTMAS STOCKING

Whether you hang your Christmas stocking at the end of the bed or from the mantelpiece, Father Christmas will not be able to resist this dazzling model in festive colours of holly berry red and pine green. The stocking is made in a jolly plaid fabric decorated with different Seminole bands.

Seminole patchwork, with its intricate designs and bright colours, lends itself to Christmas projects, and if your sewing machine can do fancy embroidery, you can add some extra embellishments.

Why not use the same Seminole bands to design a decorative Christmas table runner or perhaps some place mats for the festive meal? The fabric is 45in (115cm) wide unless otherwise specified.

1 Scale up stocking pattern shown on pages 108–109 to 269% on a photocopier. Cut the stocking front and the back from the red plaid, and two pieces from the green cotton fabric. It is not necessary to leave any seam allowances as the stocking will be bound.

2 Refer to instructions for the Seminole Cushion (*see pp. 58–59*) to make Seminole bands 1 (Zig-zag), 2 (Woven), and 3 (Chevron), and to the Seminole Tree Ornament (*see p. 103*) to make Band 4 (Double jagged). Use the photograph as a guide for placing the different colours of fabric. Cut Band 1 into two pieces: one 9in (23cm) long and one 7in (18cm) long. Cut Band 2 about 9in (23cm) long, Band 3 about 10in (25cm) long, and Band 4 about 8in (20cm) long (*see Fig. A*). You can save remnants of bands to make Christmas cards (*see pp. 104–105*) or pincushions (*see pp. 96–97*).

3 Cut six strips from the green and four from the white fabrics measuring 1in (2.5cm) wide and about 10in (25cm) long. Sew the strips to each side of the Seminole bands (*see Fig. A*). Press under a ¼in (6mm) hem turning along the raw edges with a steam iron. Pin the bands in position on the stocking front (*see Fig. B*). Carefully stitch the bands to the stocking, keeping close to the folded edges.

4 Pin the stocking front to a green lining piece, wrong sides together. If you wish, decorate the strips with fancy machine embroidery in red and green. Trim away excess fabric level with the lining pieces (*see Fig. C*).

5 Pin stocking back to the other lining piece. Cut two strips of green fabric 2in (4cm) wide and 10in (25cm) long. Use strips to bind the tops of the stocking front and back.

6 Pin the stocking front to the stocking back with wrong sides together, and bind raw edges with bias binding. Make a loop 5in (12cm) long and sew to the stocking top.

PROJECT TEMPLATES

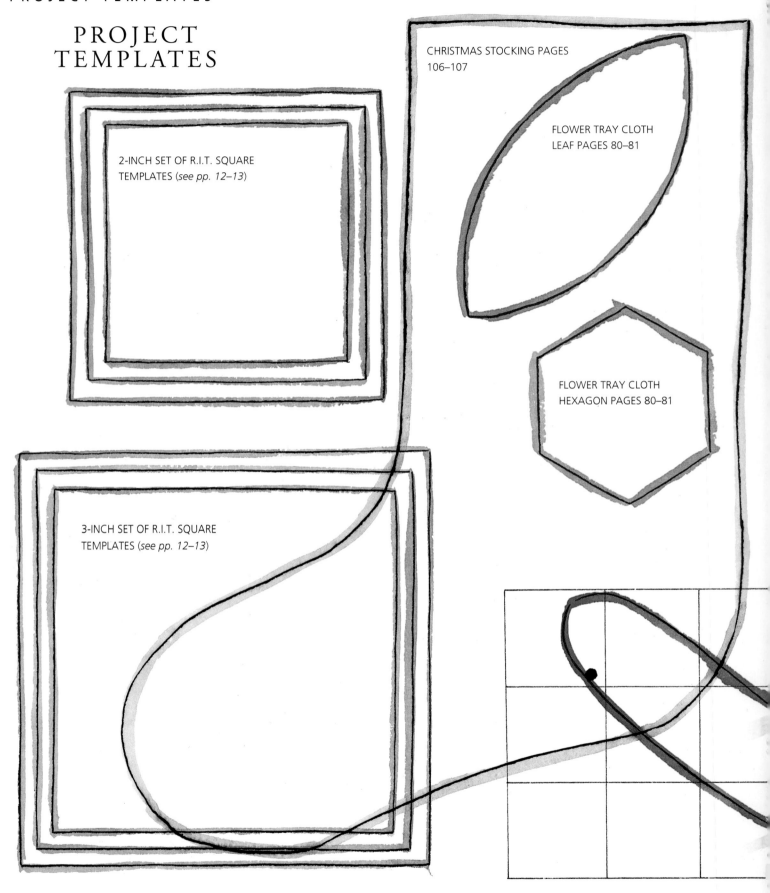

2-INCH SET OF R.I.T. SQUARE
TEMPLATES (*see pp. 12–13*)

3-INCH SET OF R.I.T. SQUARE
TEMPLATES (*see pp. 12–13*)

CHRISTMAS STOCKING PAGES
106–107

FLOWER TRAY CLOTH
LEAF PAGES 80–81

FLOWER TRAY CLOTH
HEXAGON PAGES 80–81

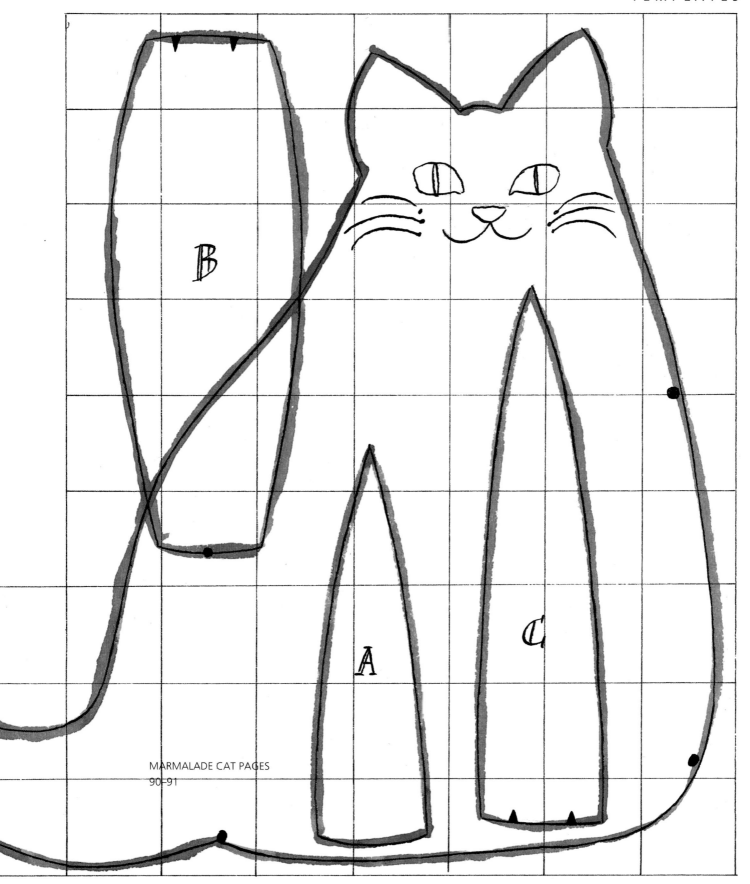

B

A

C

MARMALADE CAT PAGES
90–91

INDEX

ACKNOWLEDGMENTS

THE PUBLISHERS AND AUTHOR WOULD LIKE TO THANK THE
FOLLOWING PEOPLE AND ORGANIZATIONS FOR THEIR GENEROUS HELP AND SUPPORT IN THE PRODUCTION OF
THIS BOOK:

SUPPLIERS OF ACCESSORIES AND PROPS

WILLIAM MAKOWER

(*Donated fabric for Morgan's Gardens Cushions pp. 56–57*)

JOHN KALDOR, THE MANUFACTURERS OF FABRIC DESIGNED BY AMERICAN TEXTILE DESIGNER NANCY CROW

(*Supplied fabric for Trip-around-the World Throw pp. 36–39*)

W WILLIAMS LTD, DISTRIBUTORS OF "HEAT'N'BOND" IRON-ON FLEXIBLE VINYL

(*Supplyied vinyl for Ivy Apron on pp. 88–89 and Breakfast Set on pp. 92–93*)

SONYA MOORE, BLUEPRINT, HASLEMERE, SURREY

(*Supplied picture frame for Quilted Amish Picture on pp. 82–83*)

THE SHAKER SHOP, 25 HARCOURT STREET, LONDON W1H 1DT

(*Supplied props for photographs on pages 29, 89, 104/105, and 107, tel: 0171–724 7672*)

SPECIAL THANKS TO

KARIN ROUND WHO DESIGNED THE NINE-PATCH QUILT (*see pp.28–29*),THE FOUR-PATCH QUILT (*see pp. 24–25*),
STRIPPY SILK WAISTCOAT AND STRIPPY CLUTCH BAG (*see pp. 64–65, 66–67*)

SHARON DARGE WHO DESIGNED THE CRAZY PATCHWORK WAISTCOAT AND THE DOROTHY BAG

(*see pp. 74–75, 76–77*)

EVELYNE MITCHELL FOR HAND QUILTING ON QUILTED AMISH PICTURE (*see pp. 82–83*)

PATSY NORTH FOR EDITING AND CHECKING PROOFS

KATHIE GILL FOR INDEXING

SANDRA AND PETER, GARY AND HEATHER AND KEN AND PRUE

FOR THE USE OF THEIR HOMES FOR PHOTOGRAPHY

USEFUL ADDRESSES

FABERDASHERY (PROPRIETORS: TINA EALOVEGA AND KARIN ROUND)

1 MIDHURST WALK, WEST STREET, MIDHURST, WEST SUSSEX GU29 9NF

(*Suppliers of patchwork material, rotary cutting eqipment, R.I.T. Square templates, iron-on vinyl and other supplies
for patchwork as well as kits for making up many of the projects in this book. There is a mail-order service and also
classes in patchwork, tel: 01730 817889*)

THE ARTFUL PARLOUR, MIDHURST WALK,

WEST STREET, MIDHURST GU29 9NF

(*"Stiffy bow solution" stockist [see pp. 100–101], tel: 01730 815085*)

BIBLIOGRAPHY

GREIDER BRADKIN, CHERYL, *BASIC SEMINOLE PATCHWORK*,
LEONE PUBLICATIONS 1990
DOAK, CAROL, *EASY MACHINE PAPER PIECING*, THAT PATCHWORK PLACE 1994
HARGRAVE, HARRIET, *HEIRLOOM MACHINE QUILTING*, C&T PUBLISHING 1990